Finding the Peace

A Journey to Wholeness

Janie Pfeifer Watson

Janie Pfeifer Watson
Wholeness Healing Center
2608 Old Fair Road
Grand Island, Nebraska 68803
janiepw@wholenesshealing.com

Graphic design by Susan Cohen

ISBN: 978-1-4636606-1-1

Library of Congress Control Number: 2011911203

This book is dedicated to my grandchildren,
Madilyn, Maclane, and Aiden,
who keep me present in the moment.
You are a source of endless joy.
I am not the same person since you came into my life.

World Universe

I'm here
Where's the band?
I don't hear the music
Doesn't someone want to dance with me?
Let's celebrate . . .

There is no music
There is no band
The dance is within
And I'll have to practice
The steps with me . . .

It's okay, world—
Join me when you can
In the meantime I'll practice my dance
And know the steps
That go with my tune within—
For truly,
I cannot share the music
Or dance
Until I can do my part
Of the dance steps to my very own tune!

Contents

Preface

I first decided to write this book as I worked with clients in my therapeutic practice over the years. They often came in with depression, anxiety, or other difficulties that left them feeling hopeless. In my own experience of conquering depression, I knew that there was hope, and that they could heal and find peace. Sometimes I would share parts of my own journey to let them know that they could find their way out of the black hole. As I wrote, the book evolved. It became more about how we can navigate through our difficult times and change our lives by looking at situations in a different way.

I live with the premise that life has a perfect order, that I am exactly where I need to be at this moment. I didn't always believe this, but through my journey I have been blessed with the gift of being able to see how the pieces of my life actually fit together. Each event or hardship became a stepping-stone in my growth, training me and preparing me for the next phase of my life. The perfection of how my life has played out has been beyond anything I could have come up with, had I tried to map out my life on my own. My perceived negative moments and painful experiences provided the opportunities I needed to find myself by digging deep and touching my soul. The gift of finding myself, developing who I was, and stepping into this person fully is the real story.

When we can grow through our difficult times, we have used our experience for something bigger and better. My hope is that readers will be able to understand their own stories and use their challenges as a path to finding the perfection in their lives.

Chapter 1

Vision Quest

Finally the time had come. Laughter. Fear. Joy. I didn't know what to expect. Sitting in the grass watching the Medicine Woman head back toward the campsite, I inhaled deeply. She disappeared into the thicket of trees. I was alone. My heart skipped a beat.

I scanned the vast horizon; against it, I was a mere speck. I sat within the perimeter of my vision quest space: eight foot by eight foot. Walking the Ohio land with Seanne, Loyie, Jamie, and Vicki—very close friends who would be my supporters—and the Medicine Woman, I had chosen the site that very morning. It was my sacred space. I had walked silently, reverently, allowing myself to become aware of the surroundings, to feel all the nuances, so as to hear the call from the land where I was to be for the next three days. Only the Medicine Woman and I knew what location I finally selected.

The space was waiting for my arrival, welcoming, almost as if I were coming home. I felt ready to move forward with my vision quest.

On one side, my view was a line of majestic trees forming a shelterbelt in the distance. Beyond those trees was a forested area. On the other side, close to the boundary of my space, were two small, graceful evergreens that seemed to be standing guard for me. Their close shelter helped me feel safe and less vulnerable, yet I could still enjoy the openness that allowed me to see the rolling hills for miles. My space was green, carpeted with tall wild grasses that were soft and inviting to the skin. Scattered about, but close, were wildflowers: white, purple, red, yellow.

I would be on this hill, by myself, for the next three days. Just me, my soul, and God. I tried to justify the intrusive feelings of concern by telling myself, "Who wouldn't be anxious under the weight of being so alone?"

I was ready. At least I thought I was. I had come a long way; there was a time when I would never have considered such a quest. I had worked hard these past ten years to get acquainted with myself and knew that my choice to sign up for this adventure meant I had arrived in some strange way: arrived at being accepting of myself and willing to sit by myself—alone—for three days. The planning had been intense over the last year, and these next three days would be the final step.

The first twenty-nine years of my life had centered on the opposite—avoiding myself at all costs, keeping so busy that there was no time to be with myself—to the point of almost entirely losing myself. My "self" had not taken kindly to the ignoring and the running that had become my way of life. At twenty-nine, I found myself in pain, a pain I can still touch and feel. Left with no choice but to be with myself, no place to run, I *had* to look myself in the eyes. I did it kicking and screaming, resisting every moment. It was an agonizing opportunity and now, in retrospect, I realized that the whole experience was a gift, a gift of my "self" to myself.

I couldn't help but wonder how this time might be different. I certainly wasn't resistant to it. I had signed up with eagerness to do this vision quest. But I also knew that many things happen to those on the hill; I had heard stories about vision quests over the years.

The solitude of the hill was further heightened by the absence of the comforting companionship of food. Nothing to eat for three days, no water the first day, and then only water the second and third days. It seemed an important part of the ritual, an emptying of the vessel; I would be as empty as the space where I now stood.

I like food. As a young child, I started using food for comfort, and as a result had always struggled with weight issues. Yet, as much as I loved to eat, I knew that abstinence from food encourages the quietness of the body. And a quiet body allows the mind to listen to the soul without distraction; the emptiness of the stomach can allow the spirit to be filled. There is an empowerment in it, a sense that within you is something much stronger, much sturdier than the strength your body receives from the food, something even more nourishing than food.

Fasting rituals date back thousands of years in almost all religions. So there must be something to letting go of the physical desire to eat and drink, letting your body empty itself to be a vessel filled with Spirit as Spirit sees fit. It is a way of putting the body in its place, telling it to be still and letting spirituality carry the way. This was the point of the vision quest: giving the body the directive of being submissive to Spirit, letting go of the physical to allow the spiritual to be heard. But I was apprehensive. What if I was one who heard nothing from Spirit? What if there was much to hear?

Spirit in the Native American tradition is analogous to life force, God, or higher power. I liked using the word *Spirit* because it didn't carry imagery that would get in the way of my openness. My history had taught me that God was hierarchical, and at times, somehow unreachable, being outside of myself. However, Spirit carried no past connotations, so the word allowed me to formulate the concept of God in a new and more loving way.

During the year of preparation for the vision quest, I had endured days of fasting from certain toxic foods and drinks: a slow but steady elimination of red meat, sugar, caffeine, and alcohol. The longer I stayed clear of these substances, the less I craved them, and the more balanced my body felt. I was able to let go of my morning coffee. I didn't need a nightly sweet or carb fix. I had come to find a balance in using food appropriately for physical nourishment. My body seemed content.

But it wasn't the absence of food that was now at the root of my worry. It was the water. I was attached to the idea of having my water; after all, weren't we taught we must have water to survive? I swallowed, checking to make sure I wasn't too dry yet.

It had taken me many years to learn that my thoughts affected my feelings, and that I could control those thoughts. I wasn't going to get tied up in old patterns now. I wanted to contain my feelings of vulnerability while I could still control my thoughts and feelings around this issue of having little water.

Another challenge—minor, but still one that caused me discomfort—was that I wasn't able to bring those special items that may have provided a cloak of solace: books and my journal. Books have always offered me a means of escaping from the present. Journaling had been part of the path to my soul, to my "self," to learning about me, to finding me, to creating me. It offered me a medium to learn how I felt, what I needed or wanted, or what I was avoiding. It gave me clarity.

My journal was a luxury I could have sunk into, but the Medicine Woman had said it wasn't part of the things I could take. Perhaps it could be used as an escape from the present, or maybe it was time to learn to write to myself in a new way. But without it, I felt stripped, bare, and yes, vulnerable. I felt exposed.

I did have the shelter of my sleeping bag and a tarp to protect me if it rained. A friend of a friend had lent me the tarp; both these women were in the circle who studied under the Medicine Woman. Over the years this tarp had accompanied many women to the hill. There was some satisfaction in having it with me, as if it held the energy of the other women who had made this same journey. I felt as if I had a wise soul with me.

I knew it would rain; whenever the Medicine Woman was around, it always rained. She commanded the process of looking within, and the rain merely provided an outward symbol of the thoughts and feelings that were no longer serving me. It also served to cleanse if and when I chose to release those patterns of thought and feeling.

So the tarp was on the list of must-haves. It carried not only the physical ability to protect me from the rain that might fall but also the emotional protection, the covering up if I felt too vulnerable, too stripped. It carried the wisdom of protecting me from the downpour of negative thoughts and feelings that can certainly accompany time spent out on the hill. It also carried the freshness of something that had been cleansed in a downpour. Just as the landscape presents with a freshness and vividness of color as it drinks the much-needed rain, so too can we find a purification of the soul by the cleansing of our thoughts and feelings. Yes, the tarp provided me with much more than it appeared to.

There was another layer of support, unseen to me presently up here on the hill, but still there. Four of my closest women friends were down at the campsite, keeping watch at the fire with prayer and vigil. Each of us, as we worked with the Medicine Woman, knew what might be in store for the time with her—rain.

And before our campsite was even unpacked, we were reminded. It was a beautiful, sunny day, and we were euphoric with the fresh air, the slight breeze, and the sight of the autumn leaves.

Our supplies had been shipped to the landowner's home. After arriving, my friends and I had hauled all the boxes out to our chosen campsite, probably a good half mile or so. We worked well as a team, excited for the next few days that would unfold with the yet-untold adventure.

The boxes and our luggage stood out of place against the backdrop of nature's scenery. We had chosen an area in a valley surrounded by trees. The green fields within the clearing beckoned us to come and rest there. The area was separated from the surrounding forest by a natural border of mossy green fern. Within the clearing was enough room for the tents and the campsite.

Each supporter had her own tent, as did the Medicine Woman and I, so there were six tents to be set up. The group also needed food allocations and a kitchen site to be designated under its own shelter (the supporters would be eating for me), camping chairs to be arranged by the fire pit, supplies for gathering and cutting wood, a shower area with solar water containers to which soap and other supplies were added, toilet tissue, clothing and bedding supplies, a trash area and its needed supplies, and the supplies for the sweat lodge and prayer rituals.

We were as methodical as possible in dealing with the disarray as we opened all the boxes and unloaded the tent supplies. We were on a mission to get the campsite set up before dusk.

Planning the details had been a bit overwhelming: making sure we had extra parts for the lanterns in case they were broken in shipping, matches, gloves for gathering wood, rain gear and rain boots, flashlights . . . The list had seemed to go on forever as I prepared to have the supplies shipped out. But the planning seemed to solidify my illusion of having some control, even though I would not carry most of these things to the hill.

In the midst of our systematic and preoccupied work, large raindrops suddenly dotted the boxes and the tent tarps. Before we could consider what to do, the rain began to fall steadily, and within seconds it was a torrential downpour. The tents became the shelter for anything and everything that was lying out—boxes, luggage, and supplies. After only a few minutes (but long enough to get everything soaked, including ourselves), the rain stopped and the sun returned.

Of course, the unexpected rainfall was symbolic of life, symbolic of the vision quest, something I forever needed to learn: that no amount of planning ever really made things happen a certain way.

Chapter 2

The Unseen Protection

The muslin touching my skin brought me back to the hill as I tenderly smoothed the cotton dress I had designed and sewn specifically for this occasion. The fabric was organic and natural in color; its unbleached quality provided a simplicity that reminded me not to get caught up in the fine weaves. The light brushing on my skin embraced me with its softness, allowing my skin to open up to all it offered.

The dress had a high waistline and was slightly fitted around my breasts, with a full skirt that flowed down to my calves, allowing me the flexibility of sitting on the ground and still giving me plenty of cover. Its long sleeves would aid in protecting me from the heat of the day. It was finished off with a splash of color: a six-inch purple Lakota star on the right front. The eight-pointed star was soothing, and it easily caught my attention. The addition of muslin straps to my purple sun hat offered my head protection in spite of the wind and completed the outfit. In its simplicity, there was beauty.

Like making the dress, there were other tasks required during the preparation stage. And as if by magic, the outcome of these tasks came together, each intricately woven into the fabric of the space that now contained me.

In each corner of the sacred area, a willow tree reaching five foot or more had been planted. They had been brought with me from Nebraska. My task had been to find these four willow trees early in my preparation, giving me time to spend with them. In the fall of the previous year I drove endlessly along the country roads outlining Grand Island and smaller surrounding areas. And after much time and quiet meditation, I had clarity on which four trees to ask permission regarding their participation in the vision quest.

Part of my weekly regime was then to tend to the trees. I would clean up the area around the seedlings, pull weeds, and simply spend time sitting in silence with each tree. I began to appreciate their splendid way of moving in the wind with such flexibility and came to look forward to the time that I would sit down under their small shadows. It was an opportunity to leave the busyness of my work life. The road trip itself set the tempo for my slowing down, and when I arrived at my first tree, I had already begun to let go of my fast-paced, heavily scheduled world. As I sat with them, the comfort came; the tension of my life peeled off little by little. By the time I arrived at the fourth tree I was quite ready for the solitude and quietness, enjoying the moment of being with the tree. Sitting in the dirt, watching the birds, smelling the fresh Nebraska air was uplifting. There was a communing with each tree as its presence seemed to envelop my spirit, bringing out my tenderness and compassion. And at times I wondered if those feelings had always been within me or were gifted me by the trees. As the weeks out in nature progressed, I was better able to shift from the daily focus of the physical world, to access quietness within myself and become more aware of the breathtaking world that surrounded me.

I was curious about why we were using the willow tree. The Medicine Woman explained that in Native American tradition the willow tree is considered mysterious and healing. Willow energy is said to bring flexibility of thought and encourage openness to possibilities. It is said to help us hear Spirit and is associated with an awakening of feminine energies, of going into the darkness of the womb and opening us to see that which has been hidden. It also stimulates dreaming. The willow message always involves learning to trust our inner knowing and visions. The explanation provoked a deep uneasiness in me—"going into the darkness of the womb" reminded me that I would be facing the darkness of my own shadow self, alone—but I continued to take the time to be with the trees and care for them.

Along with tending to the trees, I was also asked to make six hundred prayer ties. A prayer tie starts with a two-by two-inch square of cotton in one of six colors symbolizing Mother Earth, Father Sky, or the four directions. The completed ties were placed in appropriate order on a string: yellow for east, red south, black west, white north, green below (for Mother Earth), and blue above (for Father Sky).

I slipped back into that time of making the prayer ties, remembering how the cadence that developed had offered another avenue of quieting myself within. Holding a square of fabric in my palm, I would add a pinch of tobacco, fold the square, and tie it to the string just inches away from the previous tie. With each, I said the prayer that the bundle would carry. "I make a prayer for my husband, who is supporting me during this time." "I make a prayer for my children, who are ever-changing." "I make a prayer for my grandmother, who instilled deep values in me." "I make a prayer for my vision quest process." On and on the prayers went in reverent, respectful ceremony. The pace became rhythmic: make the prayer tie, say the prayer, tie it on the string, and move on to the next prayer tie. It required an emptying of the mind that I came to fully embrace.

And although I partook totally in each ritual of preparation, I had no real understanding of how they would be carried onto the hill with me at the time—or if they would be on the hill with me at all. However, it all came together on the first day.

The Medicine Woman and I carried my supplies up to the hill in one trip. When we arrived at the site I had chosen, the Medicine Woman acted with a speed that aroused anxiety within me. She began by counting out eight big steps from where we were standing. Once there, she pounded one of my willow trees into the ground. Then she measured off the second side of the square and pounded in another willow tree. Within minutes, she had the four willow trees in place. Next she asked for my prayer ties. The six hundred ties were attached to a string that had been wrapped around a two-foot square of cardboard and carefully wound to prevent tangling.

The Medicine Woman found the end of the string and tied it to one of the willow trees, close to the ground. Unwinding the string, she walked to the next willow tree and around it to the next one. She continued until she had completed the perimeter of the square and used all the string with the prayer ties attached. There, inside the area, was to be my vision quest space for at least the next forty-eight hours. With two stones set on top of the string, she marked the doorway I would use to leave the vision quest area to relieve myself or get a drink of water. The bottles of water were not to be stored within the space.

The willow trees calmed me. There was a deep part of me that was grateful I had taken the time for these four trees. I could almost sense their spirits here with me and felt compassion and tenderness extending to me from each corner. Feeling vulnerable, I took a moment to soak it in and allow the calm to wash over me.

There was comfort in having my prayer ties with me as well. It was reassuring to think of each bundle carrying a prayer. Tied low, the string itself disappeared into the grass. Some of the bundles showed through the grass, others did not. But even those that only peeked through the grass showed a bit of color, leaving one wondering what was revealing itself.

I couldn't help but marvel at this amazing creation. My prayer ties, little bundles, lay on the ground marking the perimeter of the area. Yellow, red, black, white, green, blue, yellow, red, black, white, green, blue; over and over they decorated the space. Six hundred small bundles symbolizing six hundred prayers, each bundle spaced about three inches apart, all attached to the string that allowed them to have some semblance of order. They created the boundary for my vision quest space and perhaps offered an unseen protection. At least I allowed myself to consider this option.

When the Medicine Woman had completed the perimeter, she added a flag, a mere strip of cotton fabric, to each willow tree. The color of the flag represented the direction where the tree stood; to the east willow she added a yellow flag. As the Medicine Woman worked, I contemplated what I had learned about the lessons of the East. It is in the east that the sun rises, with a new day unfolding, and so the East reminds us of new life. It brings in healing and creativity, awakens intuition, and opens opportunities for learning. I would welcome lessons from the East as blank slates, and new beginnings were always enticing to me. Excitement danced in my heart as I considered this—a fresh new start. I was sure new lessons, new parts of myself, would come forth with time on the hill.

Next the Medicine Woman approached the willow in the south with a red flag. South brings the lessons that include vibrancy, playfulness, warmth, and understanding. It can be the awakening of the inner child. Playing wasn't my strength. It was hard for me not to be always working on something. But I knew that enjoying playfulness is certainly helpful and keeps us in balance as we navigate life's happenings. Yes, I would be blessed to have the lighthearted lessons from the South bestowed upon me as well. In fact, I would embrace having lessons easily and playfully given to me.

As I contemplated the lessons that may come from the South, the Medicine Woman moved to the west willow, a black flag in her hand. I hesitated to even think about lessons from the West, but in my avoidance this direction was most predominant in my mind. The black prayer ties certainly stood out against the backdrop of the green grass, catching my eye. Native American tradition had taught me to pay attention to such signs. Just the fact that I was noticing the black prayer ties more than the others was an indication to take note. I wasn't sure I wanted to know what the sign might be trying to tell me. The West symbolizes intro-spection, the need to turn your eyes inward and examine yourself as the sun sets and the day ends. It is the direction of sacred quests, visions, dreams, and journeys. It symbol-izes completion.

I rationalized, telling myself that we have many posi-tives times—graduations, for example—when we reach completion in our lives. Yet it was to the completion of the life cycle that my mind turned, a completion that makes me uncomfortable. Black symbolizes death: death of self, death of patterns, death of relationships. It is also the emp-tying of the old in order to bring in the new. It can be a "clearing away" of those parts of ourselves that no longer serve our souls' work.

But thinking about the death of anything, even just the changing of an old pattern for the better, made me anxious. It was the unknown again. Sometimes looking inward can mean looking at the shadowy parts of oneself, the parts one avoids by choosing to keep them in the dark. Obviously, going within, looking at myself, was exactly what the vision quest was about, so black would be symbolic of this time. But black was also about dying, which made me wonder what or who would be dying on this hill.

As I was lost in my thoughts, the Medicine Woman had moved on and was asking me for the white flag to at-tach to the willow in the north. Happy to distract myself, I directed my attention to the lessons from the North. The white prayer ties lay next to the black ties. I couldn't help but note how stark they looked in comparison. The black ties appeared as a deep black hole, while the white ties seemed vibrant and alive. The North does send tests and teaches the courage, endurance, and wisdom that come with the trials of life, probably most needed after the lessons from the West. Its lessons also symbolize cleansing, strengthening power, and feminine wisdom. North has an energy that brings balance and abundance. I contemplated how the North lessons might play into my journey on the hill. I knew that I had already had to reach within to find strength and courage to even agree to be by myself out on the hill. I would continue to need the strength from the North. I made a prayer in gratitude for the lessons that the North might bring.

With the flags in place, the Medicine Woman reminded me that, in addition to prayers to the four directions, we would also pray to Mother Earth and Father Sky. She began by turning east. After making a prayer to each direction, she bowed down toward Mother Earth and prayed. I too made a prayer as I touched the grasses and contemplated how we are all of Mother Earth, the same—plants, trees, rocks, minerals, birds, fish, two-legged ones, and four-legged ones. And as we are all related, we must respect all that live in the world with us, including all of nature. Green reflects abundance, growth, and healing.

Looking upward, her arms raised, the Medicine Woman ended with a final prayer to Father Sky.

"Grandfather Sun, Grandmother Moon, and all our grandmothers, grandfathers, and ancestors that went before us, protect this two-legged one as she journeys through her vision quest. Father Sky, carry this message to the Great Spirit for us."

I too raised my arms and turned my face upward, allowing the breeze to cool my face while the sun warmed it. I asked for the protection of my ancestors, all my grandmothers and grandfathers. The blue sky, in its infiniteness, cloaked me as I specifically called on my grandma Dorothy and my grandpa Werner. The thought of them watching over me gave me solace.

And then the Medicine Woman was done. She had completed her work. She looked at me and said, "There are three things you must remember. If the third thing happens, you are to return to the campsite immediately." With those words, she issued three warnings and asked me to repeat them back to her. My heart beating rapidly, I echoed her warnings. And with my final words, she quickly retreated down the path until she was out of sight.

Trying to calm myself, I turned to other thoughts. Looking out across the horizon, seeing the treetops down in the valley, hearing the rustle of the leaves with the slight breeze moving through them, scanning the sky for the birds that soared high above me, and noting the setting sun made me very aware that I was merely one small particle in the universe.

Yes, I had staked out my space, and the prayer ties were here to remind me that the vision quest was a spiritual process, and my dress was soothing. But it took only a moment of being aware of the physical surroundings to remind me of my smallness. In that moment, I found anxiety lurking. I knew that darkness would settle in soon, and once more drama started to unfold in my mind.

Chapter 3

Ignoring the Pain

As I sat on the hill, I thought of my extended family attending my cousin's wedding this weekend. My vision quest date had been set before the wedding was announced. I was missing the big family gathering. Although I would have enjoyed seeing my relatives, I also didn't mind. I had stopped going to many family events after my hospitalization, even though I was one of the few in our large family who skipped them. Things had never seemed the same after the hospitalization.

April 8, 1987. The date is burned into my memory. I had to do it. I had no choice. I dialed the number of the hospital fifty miles away and talked to someone in admissions.

"Do you want to hurt yourself?" asked the woman on the other end of the phone. As I answered, the scene from the night before played out in my mind. I had eventually restrained myself from using the rifle. But only after I had actually gotten it out of the closet and held it under my chin to see if I could do it . . . press the trigger as it pointed to my head. I knew it could work. It seemed like such a long rifle, but I had been surprised—I *could* reach the trigger with the cold barrel resting on my neck just below my chin . . . The next question, did I have a plan? At least this woman seemed to sense the urgency in the situation.

My psychologist hadn't captured this urgency the night before. He hadn't heard the desperation in my voice: "Please help me, I really want to die. I really want to escape from this raw pain. I'm hopeless that it'll ever go away. Please, please save me from myself."

No, I hadn't actually said those words, but when you call your therapist in the evening and alert the answering service, "YES, IT IS AN EMERGENCY!" don't you think he would have enough training to know this was a serious situation? I had never called him in an emergency before. After hearing my concerns, he had merely told me to go for a walk.

I hung up the phone with an overwhelming sense of doom. He wasn't going to be able to help me. If he really thought I could take a walk right now, he had missed the message. Nine months of sitting on his couch, unloading my soul, telling him all my feelings, my pain, my sadness, my aloneness, and he disregarded this critical moment.

I had thought about taking pills, driving off a bridge, or driving in front of a truck for months now. Initially, they were only fleeting thoughts that haunted me. I tried, in vain, to resist them, to ward them off. But as my emotional pain intensified, so did the thoughts. They came more and more frequently and stayed longer and longer to haunt me. The more I tried to ignore them, the more they seemed determined to be in charge.

There was no warning. I could be in the middle of a perfectly sane moment, driving down the street, and the thought would come barreling through me that I should drive in front of the truck. I knew that if I couldn't stop these thoughts I would step into that dark void—an abyss that took away my footing and flooded me with the visions of following through. But my desire to have the thoughts stop was not adequate to prevent them from filling my mind, often at the least opportune times, when I was feeling the most vulnerable or had the least amount of energy to shield myself. And when the thoughts pushed me into the dark hole, I had no defenses. It scared me how good it sounded. Death and relief from the pain were calling.

So why didn't my psychologist understand? How could I consider going for a walk and risk meeting neighbors on the street? I hadn't even been able to take my children to their violin lessons that evening. I treasured being part of their activities. In fact, it was those parts of life—watching them grow and learn—that lured me out of bed every day. I cherished my children and basked in the energy of their young souls. They seemed to reveal the freshness of each day in their faces.

But this particular evening in 1987, even my children couldn't bring me out of the grips of the dark abyss. So my husband, Jerry, stepped in saying, "Honey, just stay home and rest. Try to regroup; have some time for yourself. I'll take them." Such sensitivity was pretty good for him—he generally resented all the running around the kids' activities entailed. This time, he didn't even nag me or play the martyr role. He just intuitively realized I needed his help.

I believe he was aware that things weren't good with me. My tolerances were gone. I was irritable, reactive, and tearful. We had been fighting more and more as the weeks passed. We had done some marital work, but that didn't seem to have an impact. My individual sessions didn't seem to make much difference for me either. I thought my husband needed to step up to the plate and help me figure out how to be happy. I did so much for him; why couldn't he see that he needed to help me be happy?

He just became defensive against my accusations. No matter how many feelings I unloaded in therapy sessions or how much I vented to my husband, my psychological pain continued and just worsened with time. The pit in my stomach never went away, and instead seemed to be growing. On the previous night the raw pain, the fleeting thoughts, and then the plan had worked up to a crescendo before pushing me over the edge.

And raw pain it was. Being alone for the evening seemed to magnify it. There were no distractions. The kids were gone; my husband was gone. I had never felt such agony. It was much deeper than any sort of physical pain I had ever experienced. My gut wrenched; a dull but steady stream of pain seemed to propel itself from my stomach into my whole body. I yearned for peace, and for relief.

But this particular evening the yearning moved into an urge for release. I couldn't take any more. I knew no one else could make sense of my hurt. Maybe I really had gone crazy, I thought. I shuddered and hoped my family would arrive home soon. The minutes on the clock ticked by loudly in slow motion. I needed my husband to get home and stop me. The pain continued to seep from my stomach. It felt like death was imminent. How would anyone survive this kind of pain? If I could have willed myself gone, it would have happened then. Maybe if I just released myself, said I was ready, I would just die. But as much as I sent the messages, willed myself gone, nothing happened, which only brought up more anguish. Despair engulfed me.

When Jerry and the kids finally arrived home, I was lying in bed rolled up in blankets. Tear-dampened tissues marked a dismal trail from the kitchen, where I had phoned my psychologist, to our bedroom, where I had taken the gun from Jerry's closet. But I had not been able to find any ammunition—forgetting at the time that for the children's safety we didn't keep any in the house—and so I had put the gun away and climbed into bed, sobbing from somewhere deep within. My crying sounded as if it were a primal call for help; its roughness hurt, causing me to fold into a fetal position, holding my stomach. Nearly catatonic, I found myself struggling to come out of the depths of my despair. I had the momentary thought that maybe my husband really did know how terrible my pain had become. Why isn't he helping me? I wondered.

Still faintly aware, I vaguely heard the kids as they entered through the garage door with their normal ruckus. There was some laughing and bickering, with Jerry trailing in behind them, barking orders to get ready for bed. Jeremy was picking on his younger sisters. They responded with annoyance and shouting. Jacqui's screams of frustration were the loudest. She was the youngest and could easily be sucked in by her big brother's pranks.

Far away in some distant tunnel, I had tried to bring myself back. My body, paralyzed, was no help to my unfocused mind. Wanting to see my children, to find out how their evening had gone, just wasn't enough to bring myself out of it. Wanting to scream, my mouth was silent; wanting to run, my body wouldn't move; logical thought felt unattainable. Panic set in as I realized that even the presence of my children couldn't help me out of the deep abyss I had fallen into, and that realization pushed me deeper into despair and hopelessness.

I sensed that this evening the kids were extra hyper after they got home, meaning more attention than usual was needed to put them down for bed. They seemed to respond to my stress in that way. When I was at my worst, they would escalate their behaviors, almost as if their increased activity would get my attention and distract me. Jerry had been as patient as he could, but he too appeared to feel the stress, the impending doom that seemed to cloak the house. His voice was on edge, and I knew the children needed to respond to his requests. But the kids were the barometer. They knew something was really wrong. Seven-year-old Jessica wasted no time, quickly opening our door to peek into our bedroom and see what the problem was; why I had not gone with them to their violin lessons. She must have decided not to come in and talk to me, which was unusual; she just quietly shut the door again. I knew it scared Jessica to see her mother so sad, acting so strange and unlike the mom she knew.

But even though I was aware of Jessica needing reassurance and of the children struggling to settle down for bed, I hadn't been able to make myself get up. I was empty. The mental strength that had helped me to keep it together every other day was gone.

That night my mind seemed to have no filter. All the bad feelings, thoughts, and beliefs that appeared to be my truth came down upon me, unable to stop. Words and phrases swirled around as they seemed to taunt me—*no good, not worthy, unlovable, disgusting, guilty, ashamed.* I couldn't fight them off any longer. And I felt a deep sadness, knowing that I wasn't able to stay whole enough to protect Jessica, protect all of my children from my inner reality. My charade was not going to work forever. My soul wouldn't have it. Pain swallowed me.

When the kids were finally settled in bed, my husband came in and sat with me. I had to tell him. He had to help save me from myself. The tears came again as the words tumbled out, and I told him that I had wanted to kill myself and might have done it this evening if I had found the ammunition.

He looked as if a bulldozer had crushed his chest. And then his face shifted. His caring deep-blue eyes went from gentleness to anger. His face went taut, with his brow creased in intensity. When he asked what I was thinking, his rampage had just begun. He started in with my being selfish and just needing to pull myself out of it. He questioned my love for my children and for him. He carried on as if getting angry would knock some sense into me. If only the anger would, I thought, as I watched his fury heighten. He seemed to reach a new peak in his frustration with me.

As Jerry raged on, I blankly stared at him, with the answers spontaneously coming in my head. Hadn't my parents already tried this tactic when I was a teenager? I knew it was all pathetic. I was pathetic. Yes, I knew the implications for our family, I thought in answer to my husband's rhetorical questions. Did he really think I wanted to be in this place of wanting to kill myself? Did he really think I didn't love my children?

He couldn't see that I was pleading for help. I didn't know what would happen if I went into the dark abyss again. I had stepped into it that evening and was struggling to find my way back out. I was convinced that the only saving grace was that I had been unable to find the ammunition. And now, I was hoping for my husband to be my path for survival. He would know what to do, how to help me, I thought. He would get it, read my pain, hear my pleadings, and save me. But he only plunged me deeper into the abyss, and his anger toppled the hope I had placed in him.

I wondered why I had thought it would make sense to him any more than it did to me. It had been this way my whole life. As a teenager, I struggled with suicidal thoughts. Jerry was well aware of my past; we started dating when I was fourteen. Back then, distraught after an argument with him or my parents, or just having too many feelings of not being good enough, I had toyed with the idea of suicide. I would take extra pills in an effort to sleep away my pain.

All my life the abyss had been there, sometimes in the forefront and sometimes deep enough to be hidden even from me. I just couldn't stop the sadness from creeping up inside me, and I would unravel with tears, panic, and those thoughts of wanting to die. My thoughts attacked me, even back then. I had spent my lifetime trying to stop the sadness. I didn't understand it. So how could Jerry?

Nothing had changed in the last fifteen years. Here it was, 1987. I was now twenty-nine, and I knew only how to go about life as if everything was all right, hoping beyond hope that the pretending would eventually stop the hurting. But the problem had only gotten worse. Yet this had been the first time I had felt like using a gun. Things had changed in a very grave way, and my fear was that my husband wasn't seeing the seriousness of the evening's events. He wasn't aware that I had fallen into a deeper hole, a darker abyss, that night.

Tears welled in my eyes once more as I brought my attention back to the person on the other end of the phone. I was deflated that Jerry, my source of hope, was not going to be able to help me . . . or that my psychologist could not tell me what to do. I didn't want to go to a hospital, but even focusing on my children was not able to bring me out of the dark hole anymore. I was floundering.

My breath brought me back to the present, back to the hill. In all the remembering, it had become shallow; exhaling, I focused on breathing deeply. I continued to tell myself I was open to the potential that lay in the experience, to whatever Spirit saw fit to bring into my life. The thoughts continued as I reassured myself: I was open; I wanted to be open; I would be open. And although it was my first official vision quest, I had gone deep into myself before and surely nothing could ever be like that first big experience ten years ago. This time I was not putting myself through the suffering of resistance. I had signed up to follow Spirit wherever Spirit led. I was apprehensive, knowing that in some way, the point of being willing to go through whatever came up could be the test. It could be so difficult; I might want to run from it. Could I let go and know that I was right where I was supposed to be? My concerns reminded me of the prayer for patience and how it could bring more opportunity to practice patience. There was a haunting thought as well, deep in the back of my mind: ten years ago, I also had "signed up" to be hospitalized. And that experience involved entering an abyss that was fraught with nightmarish moments.

Chapter 4

A Picture~Perfect Life

From the outside looking in, I had the world handled. I was vibrant, personable, intelligent, talented, and highly energetic, accomplishing whatever I set out to do. The snapshot view of my family showed three beautiful children who all resembled each other and fit naturally into the family, taking on features from each parent. With his deep-blue eyes and brown hair, Jeremy, nine years old, looked like his father. His build recalled Jerry's in each fine detail, including his thick muscular thighs and arms, which contrasted with a gentle baby face that smiled deep into your soul. Jessica, seven, and Jacqui, four, both had more of my features, with green eyes and thick, light hair that took on a sandy blonde cast in the summer, although their hair was somewhat darker than mine. The girls looked strikingly alike at times, almost passing for twins.

Jerry, at five foot ten, was handsome with dark hair and complexion and a stocky, muscular build. His very deep blue eyes set off his wide smile. He had a calming disposition and a sense of humor, which Jessica shared, and their laughter often echoed through the house. Jerry was playful but hardworking, and a man of projects who was always busy, whether it was building the perfect fort for the kids or creating a pond in our backyard for my birthday. Jacqui shared these attributes; she could lose herself for hours in a play project. Jerry was a family man to the core and just liked being home with his family when he wasn't at work. He had a strong sense of ethics and values, treated me with respect and kindness, and loved me as his wife.

Knowing that my sadness didn't make any sense according to the world's view of my life, I had worked hard to portray the happiness that others expected. When the inner struggles became more difficult, the laundry list of all my blessings was one of the ploys I used. With the list, I could set up a good defense as to why there was no reason for my unhappiness. We were the picture-perfect middle-class family living the American dream.

Our three children were all a parent could ask for: healthy, fun, intelligent, creative, and very spirited. We lived in suburban America on acreage just outside of town. The ranch-style home we had built for ourselves was our pride and joy, a recent example of our work together. Jerry and I were a perfect team in whatever project we chose because we both liked to set our goals, focus, and dig in. Neither of us shied away from hard work; we would roll up our sleeves and start in on our newest vision, full of energy and enthusiasm.

Our children, like all the children in the neighborhood, benefited from the freedom our safe suburb allowed. Most children belonged to a core group of their own age. They could be seen around the neighborhood hanging with their group, whether they were riding bikes, making an exclusive clubhouse in the wooded area, or congregating to discuss the latest troubles in school. Although they were always busy doing something, they were also aware of their mothers' watchful eyes from the kitchen windows. If something went on that wasn't right, a mother would most likely see it. And the kids knew that these mothers would not hesitate to follow through.

When school was in session, the groups would move from the neighborhood streets and backyards to the school grounds, with the parents carpooling and sharing resources to transport them to the little country school three miles from home. We were a little village raising our children together. It was an idyllic setting.

School meant that there would be daytime hours when the neighborhood seemed to be resting. But after school and during the weekends, activity abounded, and as the seasons changed, the activities changed. But even during the cold Nebraska winters, the outdoors was the meeting place for the kids.

The open lots behind and in front of our house provided the perfect landscape for sledding. The neighborhood children would spend hours riding the hills, laughing, and nose-diving into the snow. On one particularly snowy day, school was canceled and many of the kids gathered in our backyard.

My son had been building a fortress of snow. As the others looked over his work and pitched right in to help, I easily picked out his glowing face, red with the cold.

Jessica, dressed in a bright pink snowsuit, seemed oblivious to her rosy cheeks and frost-covered hair as she and her friends discussed the next step in the tunnel she had started on the other side of our yard. Each of her friends took a turn crawling through the six-foot scooped-out area.

Jacqui, only four years old, wanted to be part of the scene, and her siblings were smart enough to know that they could use her pent-up energy to help get what they wanted done. Jessica knew how to manage Jacqui, and quickly put her to work.

Snow was flying, and all the children were so busy and focused that they disregarded the cold and the wind. I intervened periodically to offer hot chocolate and give each of the kids some time to warm up. But they were a determined bunch, drinking up quickly, and heading right back out to continue.

It was on these days that I felt grateful for my lifestyle. I had flexibility and was able to stay home with my kids on snow days. It wasn't just by happenstance though; I had set out to make it happen. Just before Jessica was born, I began my custom-drapery business. Money had been tight with one child, so with another baby on the way I knew I needed to help with the finances. But I did not want to leave our son and our newly expected baby to work outside the home, so I brainstormed with Jerry.

My mother had taught me to sew, and by junior high I was sewing everything from jeans to coats. It was during our brainstorming that I remembered our old family friends who ran a drapery business out of their home. Jerry and I liked the potential we could see in this business.

I spent a week with our friend, learning to make draperies. It was the start of building my own successful business. I would meet with clients in their homes to help them choose the right design and fabric. Back at home I would figure out the bids, order the fabrics, and make the drapes. My workroom was large enough for our kids to bring in their own projects, and they did. Next to large pieces of fabric waiting to be sewn, there was often a Lego village in the making, Barbie dolls needing to be picked up, and a collection of Fisher Price toys. When I finished a job, Jerry and I would go to the customer's home and hang the rods and draperies.

The business grew, which didn't surprise us. Jerry and I shared the belief that we could make anything happen if we wanted it enough and worked hard enough at it. That was how we tackled life; if we wanted something, we made it happen.

Our family kept busy in other ways too. The children were involved in Suzuki piano and violin lessons, swimming, and gymnastics. The Suzuki approach required a parent's participation, so I was very involved—three children to practice the piano with and three children to practice the violin with, all daily—and I totally embraced being part of it. Striving to help my children be stimulated and learn new things, I spent countless hours working with them. As a child, I had yearned for this connection with my own parents and so became consumed in giving it to my children.

We also had our family projects. Jerry and I had a garden so our summers were kept busy with the gardening, and then the canning and freezing of the foods we raised. The children helped with the planting, tending the garden, picking the foods, and preparing them for preservation. It was always a family effort.

Jerry's primary job was the management of our main business, the rental of lawn, garden, construction, and party equipment. We were partners in that business with my father. It was open seven days a week except during the winter, so often on weekends the entire family would be at the business working (or playing).

At times the daily routine of our active lives helped to keep me occupied. I could distract myself if I was busy enough, and I even felt some happiness at times, or at least what I thought might be happiness but was actually relief from my sadness. I was constantly challenging myself to create new, more-complex drapery designs. Once I had met that challenge, I would be satisfied for a while. But soon restlessness would set in, and I would crave another big challenge.

When I could wrap myself up in my children's lives, spending time with them, watching them grow and develop, I could forget about my pain. They were my focal point, my driving force through the day. Sometimes there was a sense of accomplishment in working with my husband at the rental business or hanging a beautiful set of custom-made draperies. Sometimes there was even a sense of fulfillment. We really were the model American family. We worked, focused on raising our children, continued to expand our businesses in order to improve our lifestyle, practiced our religion, and strove to do good for others.

Yet there was always something amiss. I never understood what my deep sadness was about, but if I paused long enough it would start to stir. In the meantime, I just continued to act as if there was nothing wrong. I saw it as living my life while putting those other feelings away—feelings of sadness, of being unloved or unappreciated, of needing nurturing, or of wanting to die. I lived the way the world expected and ignored myself and that inner tugging. I always tried to be a good person and would do anything for anyone, thinking that in some way maybe I would finally be able to forget about those buried thoughts inside myself, earn my way out of this hell, and find some peace. But that had been my mission throughout my life and nothing had changed, no matter how much I worked to try to live right.

It was the only thing that I had ever been unable to overcome by setting my mind to it, and the situation had progressively gotten worse. Now when I went into despair I accessed the abyss much more quickly. It seemed much deeper than before, and I had no idea how to get out once I slipped into it.

Chapter 5

The Red-Tailed Hawk

The *keeeeee-arr* call of a large hawk flying above me and the slight breeze brushing my face brought me back to the hill, to my vision quest space, and away from the memories that seemed to be flooding my mind. My eyes locked on the large bird as it circled overhead. The faint *keeeee-arr* grew more distinct as the hawk came closer. Spiraling downward, the bird glided effortlessly over me. I sensed myself gliding downward as well. Downward through the memories that rarely came up anymore after ten years. Downward through the memories that I had finally packed away.

Keeping my eye on the hawk, I could see its red tail as it banked to the left. "I see you," I whispered to the bird. In the past, the red-tailed hawk had had an uncanny way of showing up when I needed to be mindful. In Native American tradition, it was thought to be a messenger awakening visionary power and bringing purpose to our lives. As it looped closer, its wingspan hinted at its magnificent power and strength.

Lifting myself up, I imagined soaring with the hawk, effortlessly gliding through the air on the tailwinds. Peering down from above, we took in the larger perspective, untouchable as we moved smoothly through the skies. I knew that this was a lesson in life for me, learning to rise above it all. It was my mantra, my commitment to myself while on the hill. I wanted to be part of the scene but also to be above the scene, soaring and gliding, easily riding the currents, yet taking it all in, all the details, all the messages, all the signs, and all the lessons.

Learning this maneuver had been vital to my healing during the hospitalization. It was the only way to get out of the raw pain, to finally realize there was a reason for it, and on a soul level to begin to look for understanding in the lesson being given. It meant taking it seriously, but yet not so seriously that I would miss the big picture—what life was bringing me on a soul level. Hawk Medicine was a pointed reminder that ten years ago, it was through the pain that I had begun to discover myself, who I was and what I was about. "I" was the blessing found through navigating the deep, raw pain.

I made a prayer to the hawk, thanking it for its gift of being here and blessing me. It was these present moments that I didn't want to miss. After all, this was the reason for the vision quest. My yearning for this quest had centered on the burning restlessness I had within to "be." It was a time to slow myself down; to quiet my thoughts, calm my actions, and be deliberate in appreciating the moment. Through this practice, I would be allowing access to my self on a deep level, a soul level, something I didn't do as much as I would like at home and certainly not for three days straight. I wanted to take advantage of my time and stay present here on the hill, and not take myself elsewhere through my anxious thoughts or worries of the future or the past. The hawk spoke again, calling me back to it, back to the moment here on the hill. I pondered the message of it appearing at this time, and what it might mean. It wasn't the first time it had shown up.

Long before I understood the Native American teachings of the hawk, it was clear to me that the hawk came as a messenger. Driving home one day after my college classes, I was taking in the landscape as I traveled the familiar fifty miles. Being watchful of the road, I also waited with anticipation as I approached my favorite trees. Daily I would send warm messages of appreciation to each of them as I passed by. They were huge cottonwood trees that always caught my eye because of their height and grandeur. They stood well above the landscape of the small town and seemed to salute the passersby.

This time, however, as I approached "my" trees, the splendor of the fall colors eclipsed the scene, preventing my eyes from seeing anything else. The vibrancy of the gold and red colors drew me in. The smell of harvest expanded and cleansed my lungs, and my heart filled with appreciation. Just as my cells seemed ready to burst in gratitude, a very large red-tailed hawk flew in front of my windshield. It didn't startle me, and I didn't brake even though I could have reached out and touched it. Nor did the hawk seem fazed by the near miss, as it turned and flew parallel with the car, with me, for some time. As I watched the hawk flying, the wind was suddenly on my face and I felt the expansive freedom of soaring over the landscape. There were no boundaries as I knew them. There was no separateness. I was not alone as I was everything: the trees, the wind, the hawk, myself. And then, in a moment, it was over; I was my separate self back in the car traveling down the highway. And I had gotten the message: I was to pay attention, to be mindful.

The movement of a jackrabbit running in the distance caught my attention as I sat on the hill looking out at the miles of prairie. Jackrabbits moving quickly and quietly throughout the scene could be spotted if I looked for them. Listening closely, I could pick out the sounds that echoed through the valley. I tucked away the idea of movement being meaningful during my vision quest and felt that physical anxiety again. My throat was dry.

A crow cawed above, drawing my attention to it. It wasn't close, but the sounds were acute, as if the bird sat on my shoulder. What was it telling me? Crows symbolize magic and remind one to look for opportunities to create and manifest the magic of life. They also symbolize creation and spiritual strength.

Crow Medicine seemed fitting for a vision quest as I would need spiritual strength. The colors in the landscape were extraordinary, which gave me the sense of being part of the scene in its beauty and perfection. The smells of the fresh country air seemed to engulf me, leaving me feeling cleansed and whole; the rhythmic sounds soothed me. I allowed myself to surrender to the moment. I knew that everything was in perfect order, and so even my memories were coming up for a reason. I just wasn't clear on what the reasons were, since this part of my life seemed to be the backdrop, a scene that had occurred, although I had moved on to the next act long ago. Yes, it had been a fierce scene, played out potently, and it affected the acts that followed. I was quite relieved to have moved on.

Then, in the blink of the eye, my memories carried me to the old scene, the old drama, the time when the quest in my life was not a planned trip to a hill, but an unexpected vision quest where I was in the midst of a life-changing drama. The drama that would strip me down to nothing but God and me—nothing more, nothing less.

I found myself on the old forgotten stage in a musty theater preparing to play out the scenes, scenes that were too intense to watch again and again, too intense to play out over and over. As I waited for the house lights to dim, a sense of dread loomed. The curtain was rising, but it was too late. In that darkness, I had already started the descent and was free-falling through an abyss, no longer able to see that the curtain had indeed lifted.

Chapter 6

Putting Myself First

I had eventually fallen asleep that god-awful night, although it was a fitful sleep, with the ongoing daytime mayhem moving into nightmares. Relieved to finally see the dawn, Jerry and I had walked into my psychologist's office right at 8:00 a.m. We knew that we were encroaching on someone else's appointment time, but desperate for help, we had turned to the only person we knew who might help us. Tersely, he skirted the interruption by sending us down the hall to our family doctor. He wanted me to be reassessed for medication needs.

Taking a seat away from the other patients, I found a private cove that would protect me from the need to put on a public mask I could not summon. Jerry followed soberly. Staring out the window into the hallway, I stiffened. My eyes locked on my psychologist walking down the hallway toward us. After a quick glance into the office where we sat, he was past us. He looked different. Small. Almost weak. Hunched shoulders. His posture said he knew, he knew he had deceived me. He had no answers for me.

Jerry glanced at his watch; 8:30 had come and gone. I couldn't help but notice his smallness too, something I really didn't want to admit. Looking around, I took inventory of the waiting room. There were a few patients sitting in different areas. A mother with a small girl, about four years old, who reminded me of my own baby. The little one sat quietly looking at a book while the mother thumbed through a magazine. Their world didn't appear to have fallen in. A handful of other people didn't seem ill but that was most likely deceiving. I looked fine on the outside too.

Neither the psychologist nor Jerry had considered hospitalization. But I knew. I knew I needed to be hospitalized. I had to stay safe, to stay alive for my children, who were my only real reason for wanting to live at the time. Otherwise, I didn't care if I was safe from myself. But I knew that it was only a matter of time before I fell into the dark abyss again and would not be able to reason my way out of it.

My mind drifted back to when I first met my psychologist; he had presented as if he had answers, could solve my problems, and he seemed to understand me. I had trusted him and gone through the steps he had suggested: talking about my feelings and being direct in my communication with my husband.

But after last night and this morning, he might just as well have punched me. I felt like the wind had been knocked out of me. In my desperate pleas for help, he had sent me down the hall for a pill, not that I didn't "want" to buy into the illusion that pills were the answer. But I knew. Last night I had been as close to the edge as I could ever go again.

His words about trying a new medication played over in my head in slow motion, distorted, making no sense but drowning out my silent screams. Our family doctor answered too quickly, too self-assuredly. A change in the antidepressant I was taking was sure to help the situation.

Frame by frame the seconds played out with the words still echoing in my head. Confused, I couldn't grasp why these two trained professionals didn't understand the desperation of my situation. Prescription in hand, I followed Jerry through the maze of hallways.

Maybe I was the one who wasn't reading the situation accurately, I thought. But I knew better. I knew what had almost happened last night. I knew it would not take much to be back in the same place again. I was two people fighting, with one yearning for the relief of leaving and the other protecting me from myself and screaming for someone to help. Yet even as I screamed, no sound came out.

The scenario seemed symbolic of my life. I often felt abandoned when life was rough. But perhaps I had set it up that way. I was the one others needed, but no one seemed to hear me when *I* was the one who needed help. It was as if they couldn't switch the roles and be there for me.

Even at this point, I was invisible. It was true. I was talking in a calm, assured way. I usually presented myself as having it all together. I really didn't know what the next step needed to be and was feeling more hopeless as we walked through the morning. I studied my husband's demeanor. There was only a shell of a person. He was going through the motions of being at my side, but he wasn't pushing the doctors. He had fled. It was as if it was too hard for him to have me go somewhere to be safe, safe from myself. Who would take care of the children, of him and the house? Who would manage their lives? They needed me. Or perhaps he really didn't know what to do.

Jerry dropped me off at home and went to work. With Jeremy and Jessica off at school, I walked two houses down to pick up four-year-old Jacqui from the neighborhood babysitter. Jacqui hit the chilly April air and sprinted for home, running as fast as she could. Out of breath, I landed at the front door at the same time she did. I wondered if I was up to keeping up with her.

Going through the motions to get myself back on track, we headed downstairs to my workroom. Jacqui went to her own little work center in the room and eagerly started her Wee Sing record; she had received a toddlers' record player for her fourth birthday only a week earlier. Delighted that it worked, she picked up where she had left off on her Lego project the day before. In time with the music, she sang, "Nobody likes me, everybody hates me, guess I'll go eat worms. Long ones, short ones, skinny ones, fat ones, guess I'll go eat worms." The words echoed in my head, and I wished that eating worms would help.

As the lyrics moved into the next song, I felt myself leave the present moment. The words seemed distant, un-reachable. "Do your ears hang low? Do they wobble to and fro? Can you tie them in a knot? Can you tie them in a bow?" Images of Jacqui and me acting out the song flashed through my head. Shutting my eyes, I scanned my feelings. Surely I could find that sense of fun, the energy that loved to sing with my children. But shutting my eyes took me to an even more distant place.

I felt it bubbling up. The pain was still oozing out of my stomach. My eyes, still puffy from the night before, felt tired, just like my weary body. One wrong thought about how I felt, and my tears started to flow. "Stay focused. You know the drill." As I picked up the unfinished drapery I was working on, I felt my muscles tense. It was so heavy, I wasn't sure I could lift it. My spirit and passion were depleted. Determined, I pinned two drapery sections together, doubling its size and weight. Dragging the large fabric over to the machine, I found myself resting for a moment. Usually, if I could get myself started, I could make myself work until I completed the drape, and before long my day would be done. This time I couldn't get lost in the project; I seemed to have no ability to concentrate. I couldn't bargain with myself, setting the lofty goal of finishing just one seam. I had to coax myself to continue, inch by inch. I spent the morning teetering between normalcy and emotional despair.

Late in the morning, I broke down crying again. And with the tears, I slipped into the dark hole where I felt myself unraveling, destroying the thin veneer that had held me together for the morning. There was no one to call, no one who could help me. I felt as if I were in a slow bleed, dying, my spirit leaving me, seeping out with my tears. I had tried to muster the energy to barricade my spirit in, but it was gone.

Jacqui was playing, trying to ignore the crisis. But she was aware as she glanced up to check on me. She was following directions and being extremely cooperative. I knew that meant she was keenly involved in the drama of the moment because Jacqui was not one to let rules stop her from her serious play. My heart ached, knowing it wasn't easy for my children to see their mother like this. Being a good mother was one thing I took pride in and yet, here I was doing the opposite of what my children needed. I was no longer a person who was good for them. I loved them so. They were my focus, all I really lived for anymore, and I had to do something to prevent them from this pain.

Fraught, I went to the phone book. Thumbing through it, I skimmed the headings; Mental Health caught my eye. Richard Young Hospital, Kearney. Inpatient hospitalization. Adult Psychiatric Services. Vaguely aware of dialing the number, I waited as the phone rang. I was transferred to the admissions office and a woman asked some questions about how I was feeling. After a bit of dialogue, she said, "Yes, it would be good for you to come in and be assessed. Pack a bag in case we decide to admit you." I assured her that I would come that evening after Jerry was home from work. I hoped he would drive me, but if not, I would drive myself. There was really no choice. All my coping mechanisms were failing me. I was being consumed. On the edge again, I was frantic.

I called Jerry at work. He was irritable: last night with the gun, this morning to the doctor's office, and now this call. He didn't agree that I needed to go. "I can help you. We can get through this, and we'll be okay," he said.

I wished it could be that way, but I knew it wasn't the truth. If I stayed home, I might not make it through the next episode that came reeling down upon me. "No, dear, I have to go. You can either take me or I'll take myself. But I have to go. I have to go for you and the kids," I said firmly.

He choked up, unable to speak. I was crying too. I didn't want to go. It was unusual for me to go against what my husband wanted, but I knew I was dying. I hoped I could make it until evening arrived.

As I pulled out a suitcase, there was a sense of panic. I thought, "What am I getting myself into?" I went through the motions, packed my suitcase, called a friend to come over to take care of the children, and waited for evening.

Jerry came home at the end of the day. As he wearily lumbered into the house with his shoulders hunched, he looked devastated. His face showed bewilderment and confusion.

I couldn't remember a time beyond the birth of my babies and my back surgery when I had left my family for any length of time. I was scared. I had given up on healing this emotional turmoil and pain. Leaving my family and my home was the last thing I wanted to do, but I didn't know what else to try. As we walked out of the house that evening, I was all too aware of the click of the door shutting behind me as it echoed in the night air.

Chapter 7

The Check-In

It was all a blur: leaving the kids, the drive down to the hospital, arriving. In the quiet of the night, I was only too aware of the hollow in my stomach, deep and raw as if I had bled internally from a life-threatening wound that could not heal. I had truly expected the nurses to take one look at me, grab a tourniquet, and attempt to stop the bleeding. But there were no nurses. As we entered through the sliding doors that opened automatically, a lone person sat at the desk, with a headset on. She greeted us and then promptly asked us to take a seat. We sat in the area right by the front door.

It wasn't what I expected; it looked more like a large, spacious doctor's office than a hospital. The waiting area was made up of several conversation areas created by two chairs and two couches pulled together and facing each other. Sitting there, I tried to get a feel for what kind of place, what kind of experience this would be. The place didn't smell like a hospital. The chairs and couches, though comfortable, were an obvious attempt to make an institutional setting feel homey.

Being asked to wait there instead of being escorted to a private area was already a disappointment. Sitting by the door, waiting with Jerry, was difficult. I wanted to run, leave. With no one paying any attention to us, we could easily have slipped out the door. No one would know we had been there and left. There was still time.

But instead, we sat there without speaking or moving. Panic and fear had settled into my bones. A glance at Jerry led me to believe that he couldn't move either; he seemed frozen and wore a pained grimace. Side by side we waited silently.

Finally, after twenty minutes or so, a woman came out and called my name, and we followed her to the admissions office, a small room just down the hall. She took a seat at her computer and asked us to sit across from her desk. She asked me a series of questions as she typed the answers into the computer. We began to make our way through a stack of forms. From time to time, she would glance up at us to clarify an answer. I was keenly aware of other staff walking through the office as I tried to answer the questions privately. If someone entered, I stopped the conversation and waited.

Between the serious questions, the woman used chit-chat to pass time. But how would I know how nice it was outside? What did I even care? I just didn't have the energy to play the required role. I didn't feel like being nice and chatty. Jerry certainly wasn't in the space to be conversational, although he helped keep up the pretense by answering her questions.

Phone calls continued to come in, preventing me from going into the feelings surrounding the information. At some point she called the psychiatrist; yes, he concurred, I did need to be admitted tonight. It was only minor progress in the process. No one seemed vested in getting us through this initial phase; the small tasks seemed to take hours as we robotically followed the admissions person, answered questions, sat in office after office waiting until someone else came to ask us more questions and fill out more forms. We were guided from one department to the next, telling the story of the preceding night's difficulties to one person after another: the admissions staff member, a social worker, a psychiatrist, a nurse, all over again, answering the same questions and giving the same life history, filling out paperwork, and talking about insurance and payment expectations.

My story started to seem like it was a medical history that needed only to be checked off. Yes, I had been depressed for years. No, I didn't know if it ran in my family. No, no one in my extended family had ever been hospitalized for depression, except for a cousin. Everything was handled in a matter-of-fact way. Why didn't they all come into the room so I could tell my story once—and tell them that I had just left my three young children because I needed help *now*?

I felt as if I was in a nightmare, but I was very awake this time. I needed to alert someone that I needed help, but I was unable to get anything out. I would open my mouth wanting to scream at each of them, tell them this process could wait, that I needed help now, but there was no voice.

No one around me seemed aware of my difficulty, my fear, my pain, my sense that I might die at any moment. This was a business, after all. They had their job to do and that was what they did. It was just a normal workday for them. Phone calls came in to interrupt the interviews, conversations between colleagues were carried on as if we were invisible, and time seemed not to matter as they had the whole shift to get me admitted. Jerry and I weren't really conversing; there was no sense in bringing up the obvious. We were uncomfortable, felt like just pieces of merchandise, and definitely didn't feel understood. But we were here now.

Finally, we were taken to "the unit." I felt hopeful that this was where we would start to get some help; someone would understand the severity of the situation. When we walked into the unit for acute care, the door shut behind us, locking us in, announcing to the ward that someone new had arrived. People were lounging on the couches or gathered at tables, playing cards, writing, and visiting with family. Some looked odd, a bit off; others looked normal, even kind. I felt as if all eyes were on me, trying to figure out the new specimen who had arrived. I could almost hear their thoughts: "What are her issues? She doesn't look like she has any problems."

Jerry stood by me. I sensed that the hair on his neck was raised. He was not about to let anyone hurt me. The smell of testosterone coming alive inside him seeped out. I could tell what he was thinking: "This isn't good. I am *not* leaving my wife here. She isn't safe. No one is really paying attention to what she's saying. How can I leave her here and assume they'll finally understand what she's trying to tell them? I can watch her better at home, keep her safe, and she won't have to be in this strange place, with these strange people. I am *not* leaving her here."

A nurse took my suitcase and carried it to the nurses' station, which was partitioned off from the larger area by glass windows. We were left standing there at the door to the station. Eyes stared, watching a procedure that was new to us. When the nurse opened my suitcase in full view for everyone to see, my breath left me; I was mortified. Studying my belongings, which were neatly packed into coordinated piles, she started going through them. I couldn't think. My husband stepped in: "Is there a problem here?"

"No, no problem," the nurse had answered, oblivious to our lack of understanding of the process. She continued to rummage through things, taking out my belts, curling iron, hair dryer, razor, makeup, and whatever else she seemed to want out of the suitcase.

After what felt to be an eternity, she finally looked up at us. "We have to take anything out that might be a suicidal weapon," she coldly explained. My heart pounded. Everyone nearby had heard her. Now they all knew. Tears welled up as my throat became dry, and I thought I was going to choke. I struggled for breath and tried to maintain an exterior of calmness—and failed miserably.

I heard a whisper from someone in the group, a comment on how unbelievably many clothes I had. I felt the blood rush to my face as a slow flush displayed my embarrassment. How humiliating to have my personal belongings, my clothing, out for the rest of the world, especially this world, to see. I wanted to keep myself locked away from all these people, not ripped open for the vultures to come in and pick at. I wasn't ready for this. But I wasn't able to fight it either. There was nothing left in me.

The nurse continued to sift through my belongings. To Jerry she stated, "You can leave now if you want. We can take care of the rest of what needs to be done." The tears that had been kept in check when we entered the unit suddenly flooded down my face. "Well," I thought, "now you've really done it. Welcome to the psych ward."

Jerry didn't just turn around and leave when the nurse instructed him, and for that I felt a huge sense of relief. He stood right by my side. I noticed that he had become quieter, even more sullen. His face was twisted in pain as if he had seen me hit by a vehicle, lying dead on the road, and was unable to bring me back. Grief was setting in; he felt the loss of his wife and mother of his children to this situation. A rather cautious person, he wasn't one to jump into the unknown. He was struggling to gain some sense of power, some control, but he couldn't seem to get his footing. This experience, this place, was so foreign to him; his wife's difficulties seemed beyond his ability to understand, much less resolve; he didn't know what to do or how to do it. But he did know he wasn't leaving just because someone told him it was time.

Right off the acute care ward was the intensive care unit. Voices and sounds periodically leaked through the doors, although these doors, too, were locked. The voices spewed nonsensical words, sometimes yelling obscenities, and sounding scary when they came out of nowhere with no warning. I startled when a loud voice yelled, "Help me!" It heightened my own sense of fear as it seemed to be speaking for me, voicing my thoughts that I was dying.

The nurse couldn't help but notice when I jumped. Seemingly compelled to explain the noises, she commented, "That ward is for the people who aren't safe enough to be in this ward." She continued to rummage through my clothes.

I was grateful not to be on the other side of those doors. "Oh, thank God, I'm not in that ward," I said. But I had thought otherwise: "I probably should be in that ward." I wasn't safe from myself and I knew that. I felt extremely vulnerable; my knees became weak, barely able to hold me up any longer. I was leaving the safety of my home and the support of my husband in the hope that these people could help. What if, like my psychologist, they didn't know how to help? Would I have trouble getting out of this place? Earlier in the day, it had made sense that they might know how to help someone with my problems; it was severe depression, they said, but now I didn't know. They didn't appear to understand me at all. I didn't have any sense that they were any more on top of this issue and my difficulty than my psychologist, my doctor, my husband, or I was.

Jerry became more agitated as he watched the procedure to admit me to the ward. He appeared to be stunned, not knowing what to do. His face seemed mixed with feelings of anger, worry, and uncertainty. He obviously needed more information, more understanding of what was happening here, and he began to ask questions: How long will she be here? When can I visit? Can I call her?

They had no information, no answers for him. He looked as though he needed a tourniquet too. I could see it, yet it seemed to be unnoticed by the professionals. It had always been my job to take care of him just as it was his job to take care of me. We had a finely choreographed dance in that way. I could read his pain, but no one else seemed to notice that he too needed emergency care.

Briefly, I wondered if he would have the strength to help himself. What would he do now? I knew I was his love, his life. I knew he felt, on some level, that I was abandoning him. Guilt tried to creep in, but mostly I felt empty and unable to muster the energy to care. I hoped he could save himself; I needed all my energy to figure out if I could save me.

He gave me a bear hug as if he was never going to let go, kissed me on the lips, murmured that he loved me, then turned and left. The door shut behind him.

A deafening silence filled my head, with only the echo of the door clicking shut, calling up the sound of the doors that had clicked shut as I left my home and as I was admitted to the unit. But this time, the clicking left me standing there alone, with the cold eyes of the patients staring through me and no place to go.

I slept fitfully that night, between tears and nightmares. When I did fall into a deep slumber, I was awakened by the echoing click of all the doors that had been shut on me that night, an echo that reverberated though my head and gave me a profound headache. This was the end. There was no going back. The door had shut.

Chapter 8

Giving and Guiding

Almost jolted into reality by the sun hitting my eyes, I came back to my moment, back to the hill. Lying on the quilts that I had prepared for the quest, allowing my body to sink into softness, watching as birds soared overhead, I focused on calming my breath. The clear blue sky extended into infinity as fresh air filled my lungs, stretching them beyond their normal capacity. This setting seemed light-years away from my life of ten years ago. Somewhere between then and now, life had shifted for me. Just taking the time to do this quest for myself, this spiritual journey, was a testament to how far I had come.

Vision quests are steeped in tradition, and as I reviewed my past year, I knew only too well how much of my time had been structured around the learning and preparation for this moment on the hill. Along with making prayer ties, tradition encouraged making two quilts, each with a Lakota star. These were the very quilts that I sunk into as I watched the sky overhead. One quilt would go home with me at the end of the quest, and the other would be bestowed on the Medicine Woman as a giveaway.

Giveaways are part of every Lakota ceremony: the more important the ceremony, the bigger the giveaway. At Lakota weddings, after the guests are well fed, the bride and groom honor each one by calling the guest forward to be gifted with a personally created giveaway. And likewise, when someone makes a vision quest, it is customary for giveaways to be offered to each person who supports the process. The most significant giveaway for the Lakota people is a Lakota star quilt. It can be traced back to when missionaries arrived on the Plains in the 1880s and taught the Indians how to quilt. Quilts then began to replace buffalo-hide giveaways in these traditions. Often some form of the Lakota star was artistically depicted on the giveaway.

The Lakota star represents the morning star and has been perfected over the generations by the women who have quilted it. But even before quilting, this pattern had been in the Lakota tribe for generations. It was used to decorate the animal skins for teepees, shields, clothing, and moccasins.

The star has become a creative depiction of Lakota sacred heritage traditions. It symbolizes a Lakota belief that dates back to early times when the Plains Indians practiced a reverence for the heavenly bodies and a religious observation of the stars. They believed that all things happening on earth had a connection with one of the constellations in the sky and that the Great Spirit had given the stars power to watch over humans on earth and to impart spiritual blessings to them.

The morning star, which shines brightly in the east before the sun rises, is said to announce the coming of light; it is called the bringer of the dawn, and it leads to understanding. It also symbolizes immortality. The belief was that if you saw the morning star, the Creator had given you another day to live and you would be safe that day. The star quilt is given today symbolizing this belief.

In talking with the Medicine Woman about quilts, I kept visualizing a quilt that seemed to be calling me. It was purple, my favorite color, with a Lakota star made up of a palette of colors: yellows, oranges, reds, and purples. The center of the star, a circle, was a pale yellow that evoked an openness drawing me in, calling me to shelter and safety, and embracing me with a sense of warmth. As we spoke, this quilt seemed to already be sitting with me, offering itself to my process in this vision quest journey. It was soothing.

But I needed to see what the Lakota star actually looked like if I was going to make a star quilt. So I set off to the library to look for pictures and perhaps find a pattern that I might use to create my own quilt. One book caught my eye and I pulled it off the shelf, allowing it to randomly open. The page that presented itself took away my breath. Fully covering the page was a glossy picture of a quilt with a Lakota star. It was *the* quilt: the quilt that I had been seeing in my mind's eye, with its deep purple background and the exact array of colors, as if someone had taken the picture from my mind and put it there for me to see. Moving from the darker color of purple to reds and oranges and finally to the yellow, it drew me to the center. Its points were yellow, as if the star glowed with life. From the pages it reached out and touched my heart and my soul, reminding me of the magical part of life and of the vision quest. There seemed to be guidance in the journey, and this image was just one more reminder that I was not alone in this. The book carried the directions to create the quilt, so I had clarity in how to move forward. It was then that I decided to make two quilts: one for me and one for the Medicine Woman.

The practice of making the quilts was new to me, but I quickly found my rhythm as I first made the pattern for the star and then went in search of fabric. Cotton, a natural fabric, gave me many color options. I found purple and lavender, two tones of red, rust, and three tones of yellow. Laying the fabric out from dark to light, I methodically cut out the five-inch diamond-shaped pieces that would make up the star, stacked them in the correct order, and carefully began the creation of bringing each piece together.

The task required patience and stillness. There were forty-nine diamonds to assemble for each of the star's eight points. Each assembled point made up a large diamond, which was brought together in the center with the seven other points. It was a meticulous process that required me to be fully present in the moment, paying attention to what was to be done with each individual piece and not thinking beyond.

As I worked on this project day after day, I noticed a subtle difference developing in me. I was more aware in my moments. I was paying attention to my life as I was living it and accessing the stillness within me on a regular basis. I found myself at peace and very content with whatever was occurring in my life in any particular moment.

I felt fulfilled as the star evolved, moving from one completed point to eight points, and then to the whole star. It was finally a unit, but I knew that many parts had created the whole. Lastly, the star was fitted with the purple background to make a perfect square. I loved the step-by-step journey of making the pieces all one.

The Lakota star seemed to carry a mystery all of its own, dating back to early times, and I wanted to take in all it had to teach me. Early in the journey of working on these quilts, the star spoke to me in a different way. It had snowed all day, and the wintry Nebraska landscape was blanketed with a white quilt itself. As the day progressed, it was apparent that the snow was not going to let up. I had been traveling for work that day, and I knew I needed to head home before I was stranded. I was joyful at the prospect; I felt my quilt calling. So I headed home, arriving in time to still have the better part of the day available. I put some soup on the stove, changed into a casual T-shirt, sweat pants, and slippers, and settled in to work on the quilt. After spending most of the day putting the star together, I fell into bed, ready to close my eyes and rest my body.

As I lay next to my husband in the quiet of the night, I heard a strong, quick knocking somewhere deep within my sleep. The sound didn't waken me entirely, but I was then jostled by someone pushing on my shoulder. I thought it was one of my children and responded with a "What?" while I struggled to bring myself out of my deep slumber and open my eyes.

No one was there. I turned toward the direction where a person would be in order to touch my shoulder; still no one. Behind the empty area was my closet, the direction I had heard the knocking from. The room was filled with mist. I blinked several times because what I was seeing was so odd. I blinked again but continued to see the mist. When I looked around, the ceiling caught my attention. The whole ceiling was a Lakota star. The middle of the star was centered where the fan hung, and there a dark opening seemed to invite me inside. I continued to blink as I thought I must be dreaming, but the image remained. And then I felt a deep sense of calm and a yearning to go within the center of the star to be alone; I floated there as I drifted back into a deep sleep.

The next day my daughter Jessica, fifteen years old, told me that she had been awakened by a knocking on her wall; her bedroom was next to ours. Her words served as validation for the vision—I hadn't imagined it. It hadn't even been a dream. The deep center, I was told later by my Medicine Woman, symbolized my going within myself to prepare for the journey of the vision quest.

It seemed that the process of preparing for this time on the hill had taken precedence over everything else in my life this past year. Even though I carried out my daily activities—I cared for my three children, was devoted to my husband, worked daily in my private practice (I had become a psychotherapist four years earlier)—my priority was really about having time to work on the vision quest tasks. I loved the focus; it seemed to ground me and remind me of what life was really all about: the journeying within, the crawling into the middle of the star, the being alone with myself. Just as the quilts were gradually coming together, a gradual development was happening inside me. I was learning how to dive deeper inside myself and be by myself on a profound level. It was apparent that my vision quest had started long before I ever arrived on the hill.

The past Nebraska winter we had had more snowstorms than normal. I had delighted in the snows, knowing that they held the potential for being "required" to go home from work early. I craved sitting with a quilt in my lap, feeling warm and cozy, while I quietly stitched and made the prayers giving gratitude for parts of my day, or just allowed my mind to become empty of thoughts.

My supporters, my dear friends, would come over to sew with me at times. Sometimes it would be just one of them; other times we were all able to gather. We would sip hot tea, each with a part of the quilt on her lap. As we maintained the steady rhythm of our stitching, our inner chatter would slow down, and in that quietness there was a true connecting, a supporting of each other in our womanly roles.

It was during these moments that I almost felt we were transported to an earlier time, a time when women participated regularly in quilting bees. I could feel the change in scenery as if veils were being quietly lifted, allowing us to see and remember as we sat in the same positions, but many lifetimes ago. It seemed to be another period of time in which our souls were together.

We would be congregated just the same as the present gathering, sometimes with a few women, sometimes more, and sometimes generations of women all coming together to work on a quilt. And in the quietness of the task at hand, words were exchanged, feelings were expressed, support was given, wisdom was passed down. We thirsted to listen and talk to each other and found it to be a mainstay of our emotional environment.

Perhaps even back then quilting was about much more than the creation of a quilt. It was about connecting, being with each other, having presence of the moment, and really caring. It was a chance to support each other, revisit life's events, and nurture one another. And somewhere deep within our present-day souls, there seemed to be a memory of it. When the veil would lift and we re-created those moments in the present, we could feel deep satisfaction for the connecting and oneness that quilting facilitated.

Working on the quilts became a very prayerful time. I was surrounded not only by the physical cloaking of the quilt but also by a quietness that filled the air. It allowed me to clear my mind and remain in the moment, focusing on the quilt. Or it allowed me to pray, sending intentions out as I added one stitch at a time. Often these prayers were centered on my vision quest, asking for strength, courage, and protection as I was on the hill. I spent other times in gratitude as I listed my blessings with each stitch. And because the stitching was such a slow, methodical process, there was a built-in mechanism to help me let go and be attentive to what I was doing. It was often a strange experience; I might stitch for hours and yet only a six-inch square would be quilted. Looking at the whole of what needed to be done could have taken me to a place of concern: could the task be completed before the vision quest time? But the stitching itself didn't allow for my mind to race and worry. The stitching set up a rhythm, as if it were a breathing technique that warded off anxiety. There was no hurrying this process, and somewhere along the way there had to be an acceptance of this. Do what you can do; that is all you can do. The process demanded making it a priority, and in this demand, it taught the doer how to internalize and really "live" the skill of being unhurried, focused, and present in the moment.

And little by little, each of the quilts became a reality. Even with all the hours involved, the quilts seemed to manifest on their own, as if they had been waiting for my invitation. I had only to step forward to begin the process, and they appeared complete and ready for their special mission of providing loving care and warmth to me during this vision quest. It really did feel effortless.

Each quilt became a quiet but very prominent being in my life. I had spent countless hours bringing each into fruition. And there was great satisfaction of having the physical comfort and beauty in the final product. But it was so much more than that. The quilts taught me about living. They showed me how to quiet myself and how to be with myself. And in that process much wisdom was imparted to me. They felt alive and close to my heart as I sat with them day after day through the entire year, until they were completed just before the vision quest time arrived.

With their completion came a sense of disappointment at the void left in my evenings. But the memories of the time together still played in my head and my heart. And recalling the time brought back the sense of prayerfulness, quietness, and awareness that came as a result of creating the quilts. I relished the memories.

Just as the prayer ties carried a sense of protection and love for me as I was up on the hill, my quilts did the same. I had my quilt and the Medicine Woman's quilt with me on the hill in my little eight-by-eight area. As I curled into them, I allowed their energy to embrace me. The quilts seemed to hold me, allowing me to sink deeper into that feeling of safety and support. The memory of their creation and of all the prayers that were made during the process of putting them together continued to caress me.

Bringing myself back to my moment, back to the hill, I remembered. It was here, in this place deep within, that I could be okay without having all my possessions surrounding me. I felt complete without needing anything but myself and the Great Spirit, almost as if I were a prayer being offered to the Great Spirit. And I bowed my head with reverence and felt my soul stir.

Chapter 9

Sit, Pace, Panic

I had soon figured out that checking into the psych hospital on a Thursday night wasn't the best decision. Everyone seemed busy working on getting better. The other patients were having group activities and time with their therapists, but I wasn't involved in anything going on the next day, and then came the weekend.

I did at least meet my psychiatrist, Dr. Murray. His full gray beard and mustache suggested that he was well seasoned, a man with some life stories. He had crow's-foot wrinkles that allowed his eyes to smile regardless of what we talked about.

His looks, his smile, and his demeanor all reminded me of Santa, a Santa whose sincerity resonated. He was genuine and caring, with a nurturing quality that left me feeling warm when I talked to him, but magnified my emptiness when the appointment was over.

Friday passed slowly, with me lying on my bed crying in the privacy of my room. A nurse prodded me to go to lunch. Sitting alone in the cafeteria, I was relieved not to be part of any groups of patients. I didn't want to chat with anyone.

I couldn't quite get my mind wrapped around the idea of how a psych hospital worked. It would be years before I exchanged roles from being to the client to being a therapist. The place didn't look quite like a medical hospital; the furniture in the common areas was more comfortable than what you would find in hospitals, but still had little give to it and held its shape no matter how much you sat on it. However, the nurses' stations where doctors and therapists did their charting kept me aware that I was in a hospital.

The bedrooms were not private, although I was lucky enough to have no roommate at the moment. They were furnished with two twin beds, dressers, and desks. Each room also had a private bathroom and a window. They were rather stark, without an ounce of quaintness. I had brought a picture of my family, which I set up on my empty dresser top. As I lay in bed I would look at the picture; it was a constant reminder of all I had left behind.

Then the weekend descended. I was dismayed to learn that on Saturdays and Sundays there were no structured activities, no treatment happening. Patients who were able to—for example, those considered safe from acting on suicidal thoughts—went home, leaving a half dozen patients still there, myself included.

The weekends leading up to my admission to the hospital had become increasingly difficult for me. It was downtime, the hardest time for me. I couldn't occupy myself with enough busy activities. I had the most trouble at home on Sundays because when I wasn't keeping a hectic schedule I had the time to realize how bad I felt. We would go to church as a family, giving me one activity to fill some time during the day. But it also gave me an hour of quiet time at church. That should have made things better in theory, but it actually made them worse. Quiet time allowed me to remember my pain. Often Sundays would escalate into Jerry and me fighting, or something would happen that became an opening for me to express my frustrations.

But if I thought weekends at home were difficult, I soon learned that it was far easier having downtime at home than in a psych ward. Here there was nothing to occupy me. I couldn't focus enough to read. I wasn't able to sleep so the long, dark night hours would encourage me to rise before daybreak, making my days even longer. I had no appetite so even going for a meal would occupy only minimal time. I was homesick. I missed my children, my family, and my home. The people around me were strangers and some even peculiar in their ways. I didn't want to talk to anyone. I had gone crazy, I decided. I had a perfect home, life, and family, and here I was in the midst of a bunch of crazies, including myself! Why anyone would choose to put themselves here when they had the life I had at home?

These first three days appeared to be a waste, a time when I could have been home with my children. Nothing had happened. No one had helped me. There were no new glimmers of hope even though I had taken this huge step. As I looked around at the other patients, guilt and shame cloaked me. I was like them. They were struggling too, yet they had been here for a while, weeks and even months. Fear set in as I realized it might take some time to get better. Or even worse yet, maybe I was a hopeless cause. I sank into my overwhelming sense of despair. Life seemed to stand still, with me drowning in my pain.

Jerry had come up during the weekend. His visit gave me something to occupy the time, but he just added to the burdens I struggled to carry. He was sullen, and it was obvious he hadn't slept; he looked unkempt and his eyes were sunken, with dark circles around them. His eyes, usually a clear blue, were distant as if it were too painful for him to look at me. I understood—I was going to that detached place too.

It was difficult to stay in the present. We tried to converse, but neither of us knew what to say to the other. Although I knew Jerry wanted me out of there, he seemed resigned, as if he had lost the fight. Once in a while, I would hear some words that carried a vague sense of battle and I would find myself clinging to them. I would sense glimmers of the old Jerry as he expressed his frustration over the hospital's lack of urgency, but our conversation mostly centered on how confused the kids were. We discussed what to tell them but never came up with the answer. Neither of us knew what to say.

I didn't feel better after Jerry's visit. I felt much worse and spent time in my room crying, knowing I couldn't go home, but not at all sure I was in the right place to heal. I was very aware that the children were missing valuable moments with their mother and that it was hard on them for me to be gone. And doing nothing here made the guilt that much more intense.

My patience had been put to the test. I had to get better so I could go home. I had young children at home and they needed their mother. But four days into my admission, I hadn't even met my therapist yet. Four days is a long time to young children. And as the days started to add up, my inner torment grew. This pain of being away from my children became more agonizing than the overwhelming ache that had made me check into the hospital.

I felt as if my skin were being torn from me, as if my very flesh were being ripped away. I was so close to my children. And because I had rarely been away from them, I hadn't known that the separation could bring such physical pain. I cried for days on end about not being with them and for allowing myself to be in this state of not having the stamina to do what I needed to do for them. My guilt for leaving them grew. My grief, my confusion was centered on what had happened to my passion for life. It was gone. Before this loss of zeal, I would never have considered allowing someone else the responsibility of caring for my children. No one could have ever taken care of my children's needs like I could. No one ever had—until now. I tried to reflect on what had happened to me. Where had this core part of me gone? I couldn't feel it. I couldn't access it. The "me" I had always known was gone, emptied out.

I could feel the torment, the defeat, but I had no idea how to accelerate my process of healing. Everything here was unfamiliar to me. If I only knew the rules, maybe I could muster some energy to get done in record time. I always had. It was just the way I handled everything. I could conquer the world and then turn around and start another project a few hours later.

This time was different. I didn't know what I needed to do, where to focus my limited energy. This was a foreign experience. But if I had known how to fix this, I wouldn't be here in "the unit"; I would have fixed it long ago.

Restless, I would sit; I would pace; I would panic. It all felt like a waste of time. I had been stupid to think I had to come here. But here I was in the locked ward. And even after taking this drastic step, I was well aware that nothing had changed. Even here, my thoughts of wanting to die hadn't ceased. No one seemed to be able to stop them or to ease my pain. Hopelessness plagued me.

And although I didn't like it here, the rest of me was tired. I didn't have the strength to walk out; I didn't have the energy to care about anything, myself included. There seemed to be nothing left; my spirit, my joy, my laughter, my desire were gone. I had to wonder how I would muster the energy to walk through this journey—or maybe I wouldn't. Exhaustion possessed me.

Chapter 10

Learning to Be

Finally, midway through the next week, I met Mona, the therapist assigned to my case. She was middle-aged, with dark hair and dark eyes. Softness flowed from her body's natural curves and radiated outward.

Our first meeting was difficult. She sat with me, her eyes penetrating, and allowed silence to be a friend. But it was so terribly uncomfortable, so intolerably intimate that I wanted to run and hide. I knew my defenses were down, and my whole self was showing. There was no hiding my dark side. It was out in full presence and it wasn't something I wanted to share with another person.

My eyes darted all over the room, met Mona's momentarily, and then darted anxiously again. I didn't know what to do with someone who sat with this much self-assurance. She was content to sit together, say nothing. I knew how to avoid, not interact, and I wanted to run from the room. I was afraid. But I was so desperate and in so much pain that I needed help, so I began to tell Mona my story. I started with my raw core, the ache that made me want to end my life. The ache that scared me enough to check into the hospital to make sure I stayed safe from myself. And with that I continued, telling her of the great burden I carried for leaving my husband and children in order to check myself in to the hospital. The agony I had caused them seemed more insurmountable than the original pain that brought me here. Tears streamed down my face as I spoke.

I didn't know the rules here; no one told me how to heal. But from the moment we met I began to honestly reveal parts of myself to Mona, something that I usually did not do even with myself. And so the process of healing began with my stretching beyond my comfort zone in an effort to try something different, something that might possibly heal me. I began to share my feelings, my grief, and my overwhelming pain. Mona sat with me. She seemed to hear me. She was interested enough to ask me more questions, guiding me even deeper inside myself.

Why did I feel that my family would not be able to survive if I wasn't there? Had I ever spent time with myself, alone? What was the dragon within me that I was so afraid to face? What was I so angry about? The questions ran over and over again in my mind, constantly churning.

Mona teamed with Dr. Murray, and their personalities seemed to work well together. Her presence, like his, was soothing and inviting. I began to feel like they might really care about me.

I had a daily therapy appointment with Mona and looked forward to that hour. From the first session, I began a purge of emotions that seemed to be bottomless; I had never cried so much. Mona encouraged the release of tears that had been pent up for years. She was very accepting of where I was in my therapy process. There was no judgment placed on it. I was frustrated with it. I wanted to move on, be done, but the tears and the sadness seemed to need to be exposed and expressed, day after day. It seemed like an endless pit of sadness that was easily accessed by just being in her presence.

One particularly difficult day Mona asked if I wanted her to hold me. I was taken aback—someone wanted to hold me. I melted into her arms as she moved over and held me close as I cried. After that, she would hold me daily, and often neither of us spoke. Her arms covered me like a salve that caressed me, caressed my broken heart, and began to soothe my broken spirit. No one had ever held me and comforted me like she was doing. No one had ever held me just for the sake of holding me. The unconditional love contained me. I felt it move through me into my cells; it became the connection I had always yearned for, but was never able to attain. And as Mona sat with me and embraced me for who I was, I began to understand more about sitting with myself. Her soothing helped me experience the soothing I was trying to attain for myself. I began to have a road map of what it felt like to be loved and to love myself. When I wasn't in therapy, I was learning how to put the pieces together, gain the skills to handle the world.

Weekdays were quite busy once my treatment had begun. I was involved in a recreational group, assertiveness training, a psychotherapy group, individual therapy, and biofeedback, among other activities. I was scheduled for all types of testing: psychological testing, IQ testing, and career inventory assessments. At least I could go through the day with something to keep me busy. I knew how to be busy. I was good at that. But when the weekend loomed, dread would set in.

Mona asked why I didn't like to sit and listen to myself on weekends. She said that self-reflection—sitting calmly and listening to what was within me—was part of healing; it *was* my work. I had run from myself all my life. She might as well have told me to go sit in a pool of pain because that was what being inactive brought up in me.

Sitting, doing nothing, was the hardest assignment of all. I had been taught from an early age that the more you got done, the better you were as a person. Without a doubt, I excelled at being productive. It was never acceptable to do nothing. In fact, I couldn't remember ever just sitting. It was only when I produced, excelled, accomplished a big task that my parents seemed to show love toward me. It was then that they would talk about being proud of me. It was then that I felt like I might really connect with them and feel like they loved me.

Now I needed to be unproductive, do nothing, sit, listen to my inner thoughts and feelings at a time when everything in me propelled to get going, figure this out, get back to normal. It confused me: how could being quiet and reflecting be helpful? Being quiet brought up my racing thoughts and my pain; it hurt deeply when I sat quietly. I didn't want to feel this pain.

But slowly I began to try the task at hand, to sit quietly with myself—my thoughts, my feelings, and nothing else. Bit by bit, I began to think about having the courage to look inside myself, to see what I might have been running from all my life. In baby steps, I learned that it was okay not to be productive, to sit quietly and just let my thoughts bubble up. And as I did, the pain would set in, followed by panic. And then the tears would begin again.

Chapter 11

Searching for Happiness

I sank deeper into the quilts, aware that I felt a deep internal peace. I knew that my preparations for the vision quest had been instrumental in anchoring this contentment. The assigned tasks had given me plenty of practice in stopping the mind chatter. I had times when I was totally aware, fully present in the task at hand—not thinking about what it would be like on the hill, or what I had to prepare for dinner, what had happened yesterday, or when I was going to get the laundry done. It was in those focused moments that I felt whole. It was an "Aha" moment when I realized that each moment—not just those that involved my preparations for the quest—offered me the opportunity to be whole just by being fully mindful in it.

As the preparations progressed, I began working on how to stay mindful throughout my day, regardless of the task at hand. When I was chopping vegetables for dinner, I focused on chopping vegetables. When I was speaking to one of my children, I focused on the conversation, listening wholeheartedly. My mind had settled down in its constant urging to get to work, to get going. I wasn't always thinking about what had to be done next and rushing off to start it in the midst of something else going on. It became a mantra that pulsated with my beating heart. "Now is my moment; now is all I have; use it wisely; be here now."

As I sat here on the hill, I was moved to reflect back over my life. My childhood had not been peaceful, although I was not able to identify anything that made it so. I just never felt the balm of comfort and love, and the message I took from this was that I was unlovable. As a teen, I believed that the religious path would finally help me soothe my discontent and deep loneliness. Somehow I had decided that my inability to find peace was because I was not good enough and that what I needed was to attain the peace of God. I became devoted to reading the Bible and searching for the peace of being loved by God.

At retreats, I searched for people who might support me emotionally. I especially connected with the priests who were there, and we would often talk long into the nights. The nurturing and love conveyed to me during those moments seemed to be an alien experience. It was rare to feel like someone wanted to sit down with me, talk to me, listen to me, and be with me.

I became consumed with reading Christian books, hoping my sinful thoughts and ways, whatever I had been doing to cause my unhappiness, would stop if I took in the "right" information, if I lived as right as I could by the Catholic ways.

As a freshman in high school, I became involved in attending retreats at a monastery about a hundred miles away. We had the opportunity to mix with the monks, often eating dinner with them. As I had at other retreats, I searched out the monks.

During one of these retreats, I hadn't felt like attending the activities, so I said I was sick. I had been depressed more than usual. Before I left home, I had taken several of my mother's Valium pills. I knew where they were because once in a while she would give me one to "settle me down." Instead of taking just one that day, I took a small handful. I wanted the pain to stop and thought that maybe if one helped a little, four or five would help more. So in a way, I really was sick.

The monks were so attentive. They brought soup and checked on me, and were so caring that I found solace in spite of my deep inner pain. Their nurturing helped me to see God in a different way. Maybe God would be more like them and not punish me for being imperfect, for not always doing right, I thought. I knew that if I could just become more of who I "should" be, I would find peace. I searched through my religion, going to more and more retreats, becoming involved in the Church and hoping that when I attained God's love I would be bestowed with the blessing of peace within.

During my worst moments growing up, I would ride my bike to church, two miles on a gravel road. I would pedal quickly so that I wouldn't waste any time getting into town, where I could sit in the refuge of a church pew. I was trying to ward off my despair. It was there in the quiet that I yearned to find peace and begged God to be given a taste of it.

Catholic churches often have side altars where rows of votive candles are arranged. It is customary to light a candle when you have a special need or intention. The flame represents the prayers that are being offered up for your intention. I would light a candle, knowing that it would burn for me long after I left the church sanctuary, and its flicker would give me some hope. But even that didn't help. I continued to struggle, and it was getting harder and harder to manage my internal pain. And the more I continued to search for peace, the more desperate and depressed I became.

When I was fourteen, I asked my parents if I could leave home and study to be a nun. I just knew that if I joined a convent, I would finally be good enough to be loved and cared about by someone, anyone. Living there would place me in an environment of pure spirituality. This idea made perfect sense to me. I was searching for that Peace of God and figured this would be the obvious spot to find it—in a place where women give up everything worldly for the service of God. God would love me for my sacrifice and would have to give me peace.

We were devout Catholics, and I was surprised that my parents didn't immediately grant my request. They didn't refuse outright, but they apparently thought I was too young to be making such a decision, so they just let it slide, and the peace never came. Life went on with me pretending to be fine when I never really felt fine.

A crow cawing brought me back to the present, the outdoor fall air refreshing my skin, the colorful splendor of the changing leaves catching my eyes, the softness of my quilt embracing me, and my little space surrounding me with feelings of safety and contentment here on the hill.

There was no sense in dwelling on history when most of that time had been a game of running from myself. I preferred to experience the contentment, allowing it to soak deep into my cells. It had taken me a long time to figure out how to climb out of that downward spiral, and it had been an extremely painful journey. When I was finally able to get out of the pain, it was the first time in my life that I had felt good. Taking a deep breath and closing my eyes, I basked in the sunlight, allowing it to warm my body and soul. Contentment washed over me as my painful past faded into the distance.

Chapter 12

Connecting

S itting on the hill, I thought once again of the time spent in preparation with my supporters, Seanne, Loyie, Vicki, and Jamie. As we sewed, I had felt wistful for times when life was simpler and gathering together happened naturally.

Connecting and talking together seemed to be built into the past traditions, but life changed with our society's embrace of technology. Now we are on the computer or watching TV in the evenings, or talking on our cell phones, often even as we are sharing face-to-face time with someone. Connecting takes more effort as our "modern" times are hardwiring us to disconnect.

I sighed as I envisioned more time together with my women friends, or the regular bringing together of women from several generations; these times of connecting filled my heart.

Connecting with others seemed to be my mission in life. To me, the most important part of relationships has always been the process of sharing souls: listening to another human being and, in turn, being heard by that person, with acceptance, not judgment. There were few people I could connect with in this way, but in any relationship that mattered to me I was always pushing for this sharing. I wanted people in my life to whom I could show my authentic self, people who would understand, love, and embrace me.

My heart swelled as I thought of my vision quest supporters down below, at the campsite. These were women who accepted me entirely for who I was regardless of what I did, what feelings I expressed, what mood I might be in, or what I did or did not do for them. They still loved me if I said no to them, or if I failed miserably in an encounter with them. It was a deep love that came only through full acceptance of one another.

I wondered what they were doing at this moment down in the valley. Their fundamental task was to keep the fire going day and night. Each supporter had her assigned time to be "keeper of the fire." They spent time in meditation, prayer, and mindfulness; through our spiritual connection, they were also symbolically eating and drinking for me while I was on the hill.

I was surprised that I had not experienced any thirst yet even though I routinely carried water with me. Clearly the connection was there and it was proving to be true, as I was not hungry or thirsty. Love touched me as I realized the magnitude of intentions and prayers that were being made for my journey over the next few days. But for all the mindful tasks the women had to stay on top of, they would still have time to enjoy themselves. Part of me wished to be at the campsite, since being with them was always a time of reenergizing and rejuvenating. I knew they were laughing and having a joyful time. That was just the way it was when we were together. I had to wonder how I had gone through life without them. Life had been lonely before I met them. I had been lonely.

Our coming together several years ago seemed random enough. We five, along with five other women, came together for an outdoor workshop that the Medicine Woman was leading. The weekend was spent camping together, gathering wood to make the fire for the sweats, tending the fire, running the hot rocks, sweating in the sweat lodge, making prayer ties, and praying. It was a busy time, just keeping up with all the tasks required to carry out the rituals. Each person's service was needed, and we became acquainted as we focused together on the tasks.

I had yearned for new experiences and new relationships to fill my soul, so I set out in faith, ready to try Native American rituals. It was an eye-opening moment as I ventured into my first sweat lodge ceremony.

No matter how many times I have participated in it, the ceremony remains quite remarkable, but the first time is still etched in my memory. The preparation for the sweat is very laborious and requires a commitment, but it is a process that allows for the mind, body, and soul to participate fully in the ritual.

Wood has to be collected for a fire that will be methodically built. Fifty or more rocks have to be gathered and taken to an outdoor fire pit where they will be heated up. Most are anywhere from four to ten inches wide, and they can be heavy. This quantity allows for ten to twelve hot rocks to be brought into the sweat lodge for each of the four rounds of the ceremony. Before removing the wood or rocks from their natural surroundings, a prayerful moment of gratitude is given and a pinch of tobacco left as a sign of this gratitude.

As someone new to the process, I found it comforting that everything was done with ritual. Whether the task was the gathering of the wood or the building of the fire, the steps had to be done in a specific order and in a prayerful and conscientious way. The building of the fire was a work of art. I watched with awe as rocks were layered just the right way between the logs, allowing the heat to surround the rocks as the fire burned. Smaller pieces of wood were used to create a teepee-like structure to enclose the rocks before the fire was started. The fire was built hours before the sweat began, to allow for all the wood to burn down and the rocks to be properly heated. And once the fire was started, ritual required someone to tend to it as it burned. So with the company of other women, it became a community-building process as we all had a part in getting the fire started.

Being the keeper of the fire allowed for moments of watching the fire spirits, breathing in the wilderness, and releasing the stress one brought to the gathering as the fire symbolically carried it all away. Others continued with tasks as the water was hauled down to the site in large buckets. During the sweat, it would be poured onto the hot rocks to create the steam. Between rounds, the water was passed back outside the lodge until the next round began.

Blankets were brought to the sweat lodge and draped over the willow tree ribs to make the lodge look somewhat like a teepee. In the dark of the lodge, the blankets served to contain the steam that would be released when the water hit the rocks.

As if the experience of participating in the sweat lodge wasn't foreign enough, all the women participating were strangers to me as well. So I had entered the weekend and the sweat lodge with a sense of uncertainty. Thank goodness the sweats were done in the dark of the night, so I didn't feel too conspicuous. Before entering the sweat lodge each woman was smudged by burning a sage bundle, allowing it to smolder, and directing the smoke to wash over the body. Washing with the sage smoke is intended to enhance the sweat lodge experience by cleansing the person of bad feelings and negative thoughts or energy. I had never been smudged, and I watched others so I would know what to do. Like them, when it was my turn, I stood with my arms outstretched. When the smoke had been moved to each part of the front of my body, I turned to allow the back of my body to be smudged. Then I joined the women in front of me, entering the sweat lodge on my knees, crawling in and around the perimeter.

The Medicine Woman was first, as she was in charge of the ceremony, prayer, and the pouring of the water, and would always sit closest to the doorway. Entering the lodge is done with reverence; it symbolizes entering the womb of Mother Earth. It is through that rebirthing process that one can find cleansing, releasing, and healing. Each woman called out "all my relatives" or "Mitakuye Oyasin" as she entered the lodge, reminding us that we are all related. Most were nude, with only a towel covering them. Some wore light gowns. This was a stretch for me as I was hardly comfortable with my body, but the ease the other women displayed was a model for me. I went with it, if only in pretense, hoping that in my submission I could eventually find acceptance within myself, as these other women seemed to have found for themselves. And I was encouraged by their apparent acceptance of my body, despite its imperfections.

This felt quite foreign, yet somehow set the stage for our future friendship.

There, in total darkness, we sat cross-legged in a circle as our skin touched Mother Earth. Someone was assigned to be the rock runner, carrying the hotly baked rocks with a shovel from the fire outside to the pit in the middle of the sweat lodge. It was a physically trying job; the rocks were heavy and had to be delicately balanced to ensure no one was burned in the process. We sat inside, in the dark, in all our humanness, quietly awaiting the arrival of each hot, glowing rock. Their radiance spoke to us with glimmers of messages thought to be from rock spirits residing within them. As sweet grass and cedar were prayerfully touched to each hot rock brought into the pit, lighting it up as if to say thank you, the rock spirits seemed to dance with delight.

As the rocks accumulated, the lodge began to heat up. When the Medicine Woman indicated we had enough rocks, the rock runner joined the circle, putting down the door flap of the sweat lodge, leaving us in complete darkness. And with the door shut the heat quickly intensified. Any clothing we were still wearing began to stick to the sweat beads accumulating on our skin and was quickly removed. The discarded gowns were placed above us into the rib of the sweat lodge, allowing the willow branches that held up the lodge to also hold our gowns.

I was starkly aware of my nudeness, my humanness. Even in the darkness, I felt like everyone could see me, yet I had to strip down because the heat was so uncomfortable—and we had barely begun the process. I had no idea of what was in store for me, but I knew there was no place to go, no place to run. I found myself wedged in place by women on either side of me, filling the perimeter of the sweat lodge and blocking my pathway to exit. It seemed at that moment that the only action I could conjure up was to be still.

Even after I had given myself a few moments, my eyes didn't adjust to the darkness. Unable to see anything in front of me, I felt off balance. I could hear the teasing sound of water as the Medicine Woman prepared to pour it over the rocks. But before she poured the water, she prayed for the first round, the round of the body. She made a prayer to the Great Spirit, asking for us to have courage and strength to walk strongly as two-legged ones accepting our physical liabilities and asking for guidance in taking care of our vehicles, our bodies that took care of our spirits. After she had completed her prayer, she poured water on the hot rocks.

As the water touched the rocks, steam exploded. The hot vapor filled the sweat lodge with an intensity that took my breath as it seemed to scald my nostrils; I wondered whether I could handle the heat if it continued to intensify. And in the privacy of darkness as the sweat dripped from our bodies, we removed our towels, signifying our openness to the traditions and prayers and the healing.

My body seemed to welcome the intensity with a bittersweet response; it was too hot, but it felt so good to release the toxins that had been accumulating. But my thoughts were screaming at me to get out of there. At times, I panicked and sought the space behind me to rest my head on the ground, my cheek rubbing the dirt. It was there that a bit of coolness could be found, distracting me from the fear that I could not stand any more heat and allowing me to let go and remain sitting there for the next round, the round of the mind.

Each round had a focus for healing. Ten to twelve rocks were added to the pit before the next round, with the door flap shut when the round was to begin. Prayers and intentions were given with each round, the first round focusing on the body, the second on the mind, the third on the heart, and the fourth on the spirit. As each round was completed, the Medicine Woman called for the opening of the lodge door. Water was passed around to rehydrate us, and it was then that we might feel cool air moving in from the open doorway, giving our bodies the chance to revive from the ghastly heat for a moment. When the Medicine Woman indicated it was time, more rocks were brought in for the next round.

As the rounds continued, the rocks accumulated and the heat intensified. Perhaps even the prayers intensified. During each round, each person took a turn in making a prayer to the Great Spirit. With sweat pouring off the body, emotions were released in words of prayer or without words, as we all paid witness.

I had participated with my supporters in the sweat lodge ritual before I even knew their names. Maybe that is why the deep connections were made; often a rebirth, a release, or a newfound openness can happen in the safety of the sweat lodge, with Mother Earth embracing us. In a strange way we all came to the playing field on the same level, one bare human body to another.

It was much later, after I had known these women for some time through our joint participation in the ceremonies, that I learned the details of their "other" lives, the parts that so often prevent us from sharing our true selves. What kind of cars they drove, how wonderful their homes were, their social statuses, or what kind of careers they had were not part of the forming of friendships among women in a sweat lodge.

I had not had these kinds of deep friendships in my life before this. Perhaps it was because I didn't know who I was enough to share my real self with others, or maybe I hadn't had the courage to let others know me so intimately with all my humanness. I did know that these connections were stronger than anything I had ever experienced before. Through these women's acceptance of me, my own acceptance and connection to myself became much stronger.

Chapter 13

The Generations

It was pleasurable to sit on the hill and be with myself. I felt connected even though it was only me out there. Most of my life had been the opposite; I was surrounded by a large family, often being with so many people and still feeling no connection, feeling all alone, lonely.

My family was much like many other families of our time. We had clean and well-pressed clothes, plenty of food, and a spotless home, and my parents were hard working. But they were inwardly detached, possibly because my dad had to work hard to provide for our family of eight, while my mother was consumed in the care of her six children. But most likely, their emotional detachment was more about their own experiences growing up. They were simply providing for their children as their parents had provided for them.

My father grew up on a farm, the oldest of four boys. He was unnaturally burdened with responsibility early on. He drove a tractor when he was six years old. When he was only twelve, he was left at home to manage the farm alone while his three younger brothers and his parents went on vacation. These examples gave me some idea about how much his family life had lacked nurturing and emotional connecting. But my dad had persisted and worked hard on the farm throughout his childhood years. And after all his efforts, his parents chose to give the farm to one of his younger brothers. This wasn't an easy thing for him, because my dad was connected to the earth by his farming. I wondered if my father had always tried to earn the love of his parents and if his life had been a disappointment in that way, as they had never really shown him that they loved him. Perhaps not being given the farm made him feel like he had somehow not lived up to what his parents expected of him. He wasn't the type to talk about it so I had to fill in the gaps with my own narrative. I did know that he had some resentment about not getting the farm, but he seemed to move past this with his own successful, self-made business. His anger and hurt were rarely talked about, but children are often aware of the feelings of those they love, and I had picked up on his emotions over the years.

My mother grew up in a small farm community just miles from where my father grew up. She was the oldest of eighteen children; the youngest, my aunt Judy, was actually three months younger than me. There were two sets of twins among the eighteen. Hard as it might be for others to imagine that many children, growing up in such a large family had seemed a natural part of life for my mother. Her childhood was not carefree. Instead, as the oldest, she naturally became the second mother, tending to the younger children and working to help manage the care of the home.

After she finally left to go to college, her father came to get her just days later, when a job opening came up in the hometown bank. Her parents needed her, so she packed up and went home to work and to help with the family. She was the only child of the eighteen who did not go to college, and to this day she feels regret over this.

Both my parents came from large German Catholic families. They learned through their life experiences and disappointments, and they passed down a very strong work ethic to their children. Pulling yourself up by the bootstraps and moving on with hard work was the cure for all things. This value was both my strength and my curse. Tasks or projects that would overwhelm most people were simply things I completed easily. Consequently, I would take on more and more until at some point I was utterly overwhelmed. But why did I always lean that way? Why did I push myself to the brink of breakdown?

Thank God I had only three children and hadn't followed the previous generation's pattern of having large families. I focused on the family and Jerry worked hard, but we always found plenty of time to be with our children.

My mind wandered lovingly to their births. I often told them the stories of their births, experiences that were symbolic of their lives. As a child, Jeremy, our oldest and only son, did everything with real intensity and determination; he was a strong-willed boy who knew what he wanted and what he would do, regardless of whether his mother or father had other ideas. He was temperamental, an artistic boy, very intelligent and personable when he wanted to be. But he also required his time alone and could be social, even with family, only after he had this time.

He was born during a raging storm that brought six inches of rain and flooded many basements. His birth had been difficult for many reasons. Jeremy had been stuck in my pelvis, and after about twelve hours of my labor and not enough progress, the doctor pulled him out with forceps. It was a brutal experience, and I can still see the picture in my mind's eye: the doctor would pull with the forceps, taking me half off of the table, and then Jerry, who was standing behind me, would pull me back. The two continued until Jeremy's cries finally let us know he had arrived. I couldn't imagine how the brutal force would affect an infant, and I had been so afraid that he was being hurt by the forceps. Jerry had thought that Jeremy would be killed during the pulls.

I bled profusely and ended up having a blood transfusion and plenty of stitches. My son had been through some real trauma, with his head bruised by the forceps. Jerry and I had been young and inexperienced—I was only nineteen—and the doctor never said anything about the trauma. After that first birthing experience, it was a wonder that we ended up having a second child only twenty-six months later.

Our second child and first daughter, Jessica, was born in the middle of a sunny Saturday afternoon. Though it was a beautiful day, it was also a Cornhusker football day. In Nebraska, football is serious business; most residents are either devoted to the team themselves or have someone in the family who is. Jessica was born during the game, and Jerry still comments about this, remembering exactly who was playing and how the game wouldn't come in on the radio at the hospital, not to mention that my doctor was at the game one hundred miles away and wasn't able to deliver her. But still she delivered quite easily and quickly. There wasn't a stitch needed, and as she was lying on my stomach, she lifted her head, looked at me, and smiled. Jerry was next to me and he remembers it just as vividly. It was as if she said, "I am here now." It was symbolic of her personality. She was always laughing, doing nice things for others, and having fun. She was compliant and would do whatever we asked, or so we thought, but her compliance wasn't necessarily what was going on behind the scenes. She may have been breaking some of the rules we had set up for her, but she never showed that part of herself to us. She took on the traditional female role of doing for others and what was expected of her, but she would eventually have to learn to be direct in talking about feelings and her own needs. Maybe this was something the women in my family were taught. She could have merely learned it from her mother, who learned it from hers, who learned it from hers. We could certainly follow the generations back to see the pattern.

Our third child, Jacqui, came three and a half years later during an unexpected snowstorm in late March. Such unusual weather should have given us a hint about how raising Jacqui was going to be. Expect the unexpected with Jacqui. Jacqui was also a very strong-willed child who knew what she wanted and went after it. She was emotionally intense as well, as all of us are in our family so she came by this intensity naturally. But her birth was still symbolic of her life. I had gone into false labor several times, so when the time finally came we still weren't certain that we would welcome her into the world that day. As I was being wheeled into the delivery room, Jacqui stopped breathing and the alarms went off. I had a normal vaginal delivery but the situation could have been much more serious; the umbilical cord had been wrapped around her neck. Jacqui's life was full of moments that gave us scares and kept our attention. We never really knew if she was going to put us through some "false labor" or give us real drama to handle.

Thinking about how my children's births were fitting announcements of their lives made me reflect on my own birth. I had never been told about my birth or how joyful my parents were at my arrival. I hadn't heard stories of the cute little things I might have done that made my parents smile, such as my first steps or my first words. I was the second born so perhaps the excitement and significance was not the same as with the first child, but that didn't fit into my own experience with my children's births.

I did know that when I was ready to be born the doctor was not there so my mother's legs were held together in an effort to slow down the birth. And so I had been ready to be born, to be greeted by the world, and the world said, "Not yet—we aren't ready to have you here." It seemed that this script had played throughout my life, as I never really felt greeted by the world or loved as if I were the child my parents were so pleased to have.

Sitting on the hill, it felt strange for me to realize that I did feel loved, I did feel special, I did feel cared about. My heart was full. And with this joy I also felt the sadness of looking at my parents' lives and realizing that they had never felt loved and cared about in a way that would allow them to feel connected, that they had to work hard and never knew how to sit, how to play, how to care about themselves. It saddened me to think of my own children, who had experienced my unsettledness and loneliness, and it made me wonder if they carried this with them still. I wanted to envision the next generation feeling full and loved, and knowing how to work hard, play hard, and embrace themselves for who they are. I hoped that I had done enough work and made enough changes to make that vision possible.

Chapter 14

The Feather

As I looked around, I realized that dusk was rapidly coming upon me and I needed to prepare for my first evening on the hill. Anticipating colder air, I pulled on several layers of thermals and socks. I geared up for possible rain by laying out my tarp and carefully placing my sleeping bag on top of it. Inside my sleeping bag I arranged both my quilt and the Medicine Woman's quilt. They would hold me, and that comforted me. Lastly, I tended to my altar, an area designated to hold items of reverence; there I had set out the few items of significance I took with me to the hill. The north corner seemed like a perfect place for my possessions: my sacred pipe in its sacred bag, some special stones, and a note that I had received in the mail from my father just a day before I left. This note, protected in plastic, needed a place on the altar and I had arranged it so it stood out.

As I made sure these items were somewhat protected for the night, an owl hooted in the distance. With my heart skipping a beat, I sent prayers of gratitude to the owl for making its presence known to me. I listened carefully as the rhythmic hooting continued to speak to me.

Owl Medicine had come to mean so much to me over the past year. One of my initial encounters with it came after I completed my first assignment in preparing for the vision quest. I was to write a letter to the Medicine Woman and tell her why I desired to participate in a vision quest. I had struggled with this assignment for some time. It felt as if I was wrestling over whether I really wanted to step into this and do the quest. The letter would require me to make the decision and so writing it brought up my fears. There were surface fears: whether I could trust the Medicine Woman to guide me appropriately, if I would be safe on the hill for three days and two nights, if I really wanted to spend this much time and focus on practicing this spiritual tradition, and whether I could actually stay out on the hill for the allotted time period.

Beyond these fears was a deeper issue that eventually came out as I wrote. The real truth was that I wondered what might come up for me during the quest. I knew that vision quests were set up to push us beyond our comfort zones. I feared the changes that might happen within me and how they would affect my relationship to my family, friends, and work. I knew from my hospitalization transformation that once you go through something significant, you are not the same person. And transitioning back into the family can be difficult. Family members don't necessarily appreciate you changing on them. I wasn't sure about growing and changing too profoundly, and doing a vision quest seemed to be a pretty profound experience.

After I was able to finally come to terms with my fears and made the decision to commit to the journey of doing a vision quest, I mailed my letter off to the Medicine Woman in Nevada. I was traveling for my work the day the Medicine Woman was to receive it. As I left early that morning, I was reflecting on this being the day my letter would arrive. The sun started to show itself about thirty minutes into my drive, and I was brought fully into awareness as an owl flew over the hood of my car, so close that I could have reached out and touched it. Its wingspan was large, and I thought for a moment I was going to hit this huge bird, but it passed by quickly and silently. I noted what I was doing, what I was thinking, and began to watch the birds in the scenery as I drove.

Within the hour, I had two more sightings of owls in flight. All three of these owls had appeared in front of my windshield, giving me a grand view of their beauty and their presence, almost as if they were concerned I would miss the moment if they hadn't made themselves so obvious. I was just amazed and felt blessed to have been gifted with so much Owl Medicine. I felt very connected to Mother Earth and wanted to be mindful of anything that was going to help me in this process, so I went home that day determined to learn more about Owl Medicine.

Owl Medicine represents silent wisdom, vision in the night, feminine wisdom, and the mystery of magic. Being a bird of the night, the dark time, the owl often represents the darkness within, a place where we hide our secrets. Owl sees what is hidden and is known to remove secrets. Because owls have such perceptive eyesight, Owl Medicine often symbolizes new vision opening to us.

I knew it was Owl Medicine that had helped me embrace my deep-seated fear of being part of a vision quest, and allowed me to come to terms with it and finally write the letter to the Medicine Woman. I made a prayer in gratitude to Owl Medicine being with me now, on the hill, and wondered what the magical moments or the possibilities of opening to new vision might be. Perhaps Owl would help me look inward to where I hid secrets from myself. I had learned to become keenly observant of nature and all its signs. I found it so affirming to have nature giving me messages or signs of support as I moved through life. I especially felt reassured to have nature's guidance and care at this moment as I sat on the hill to complete my vision quest.

The hooting continued to echo from afar, making me aware that dusk had given way to night. I didn't feel prepared for night to come upon me so quickly, but I held on to the idea that I would have Owl Medicine to help me befriend the darkness. As I tried to embrace the shadows, I was reminded of the Medicine Woman's words to me earlier that day as she prepared to leave me—the three important things to remember while alone on the hill. One governed my stay; if it occurred, I was to leave immediately. I knew I would be terrified if that happened, and I stopped myself from going further with those thoughts. I knew I didn't need to become fearful of being out here alone; nor did I want to.

The first warning, I knew I could manage. I was not to engage any being, which primarily meant that I was not to have eye contact with any animal, bug, or person. The Medicine Woman would be coming back to my space in twenty-four hours to let me know that I could start to drink water, and I could not have eye contact even with her when she approached. After this time, I was to remember to drink water regularly. It wasn't this warning that concerned me. It was the other two.

The second instruction the Medicine Woman had given me was that I was to enter and leave my area only between the two stones she had placed to create a doorway. I would leave only when I wanted to relieve myself or get water to drink. Each time I left, I was to open and close the gate symbolically. Entering was a step into the sacred space that separated this time from the rest of my life and invited Spirit to bring in new life. Within the perimeter was the safety of all the ancestors that came before me and all the spirits that were there to guide me in the vision quest journey. But even as wonderful as it all sounded, I felt a bit anxious, wondering what it would mean if I forgot to open or close the gate.

The third warning kept replaying in my head: "If 'red eyes' appear before you, you are to return to the campsite immediately." That warning truly scared me. As a teenager lying in bed before going to sleep, I had experienced those red eyes, fearing that they were evil spirits or the devil. I had preferred to think that I had made up those red eyes, that they hadn't just appeared out of nowhere. But now I knew differently, and I certainly didn't want them to appear while out on the hill all by myself. It was a certainty that I needed to open and close that gate each time. Could forgetting this step of shutting the gate allow the red eyes into my space?

The hooting of the owl calmed my fears and reminded me that all was in order. However the vision quest played out was how it was meant to play out. I felt a strong sense of Owl Medicine with me as I remembered that I actually did have Owl presence right there in my space. I went to my altar and picked up the note my father had sent me. It had arrived in the mail the day before I left. Immediately recognizing my dad's small and careful writing had piqued my curiosity. Inside the envelope was a small writing pad with a few pages left in it. The top page had a short note: "We'll be praying for you while you are gone. Have a safe trip. Love, Dad." I was affirmed in receiving it, as I knew my parents didn't necessarily understand what I was doing but thought their prayers were a support I would welcome and appreciate. Further into the pad I found a feather, an owl feather. Dad had arranged it carefully within the pages to keep it pristine. His gift touched me deeply. My parents had an owl living on their land, and as I prepared for the vision quest, we had talked about it. My dad must have listened carefully to realize how important owls had become to me. He had found the feather and actually saved it to mail to me. It was the perfect gift of support from him, and I knew it meant that I would have Owl Medicine during the vision quest. But it meant more than that. It implied that I also needed my dad's medicine, which I had taken with me in his note. The simple fact that he had made this gesture meant a lot to me. His note brought his presence to my space and comforted me as night descended. By showing me that he had connected to me and really heard me, his inferred understanding gifted me.

Chapter 15

The Search for Peace

After six weeks of being in the hospital, nothing had really changed. I didn't understand it. What was missing? It had been weeks since that awful night I almost died; weeks since I checked in to the unit; weeks of being away from my children—and still no peace or real desire to live. What did I need to do? I revealed my frustrations to Mona in therapy, asking her the questions that stirred within me.

Mona listened and paused for a moment, then said, "Right there is the problem. You don't have to 'do' anything. You have to 'be.' You are the gift. You don't have to earn your love, your peace, your place in heaven. You are already perfect. You are God."

What? I gasped at her words and waited for the lightning bolts to come down and strike us. I just knew that I had participated in sin by even listening to a statement that sounded so sacrilegious. But even as I was profoundly protesting the statement, something hit me right in the heart.

Mona continued, "Listen from the inside out. Don't listen from the outside in." I didn't know what the message was; Mona was talking about listening with my heart, but I always had that "clutter," as she called it, around me. The clutter was all the sounds, the voices, the thoughts that I let in from the outside and allowed to influence me. I realized that my heart was beating rapidly as I tried to decide if I should grab the journal that sat in my lap and run, or stay and let Mona tell me what she meant by the words "You are God."

I took a deep breath. "Okay," I thought, "Calm yourself. Make yourself breathe!"

Mona sat quietly, waiting for me to say something. All was quiet . . . nothing . . . I felt uncomfortable but looked at Mona as she explained, "We are fragments of the light of God. We are actually all one, one light, and we all are part of God. God is in us and we are of God. We all make God. The ocean is made up of water particles. God is the ocean and we are the water particles. God is the forest and we are the trees."

I struggled to sit there and let the words seep in.

I am a fragment of the light of God . . . I am God. I am already perfect. It was hard for me to wrap my mind around such a profound reality. It was so unlike anything I had been taught, anything I had ever heard or felt or lived. It stopped me short, and questions that I could no longer contain began to flood me.

I had spent all my life not letting in such questions, immediately disregarding them if they did not fit with my religious upbringing. But right now my religious foundation was shaky—I was shaky—and I felt desperate to hold on to a truth that would support me. I had to ask, "Is there really one religion, the Catholic religion?" "What would happen if I practiced spirituality in a different way?" "What way would that be?" "Are we lowly sinners or are we loved as we are?" "Was I really already enough?" "What if I believed this and the words were not the truth?" "How do we know the truth?" and most importantly, and the scariest for me, "Would my mother and father still love me if I didn't believe these religious truths as they had taught me?"

Fear set in as I allowed myself to venture into this unknown arena that gave me the sense of having some authenticity and truth. As I sat there, I was aware that along with a flooding of questions, I was simultaneously being immersed in childhood memories. Scenes were flashing through of those times when I did have my parents' attention. Mostly it was when I had failed to live up to the expectations that were set for me. These times seemed to deliver the message "You are not enough; you need to change."

One scene took me back to when I was quite young, probably about seven. I had been very upset about something, and I had gone upstairs to my bedroom where I was rocking in my blue vinyl chair. As I rocked, the chair moved along the wooden floor of my room, echoing the beat of my heartbreak. The longer I was alone in my bedroom, the more upset I became, and the rocking rhythmically increased with my crying. Rocking was my attempt to self-soothe, but it wasn't helping. My crying moved into wailing and then sobbing to the point of not being able to breathe.

My mother finally came upstairs, which I remember wanting very much. But she entered my room with frustration because she had heard enough. She told me to cut it out, and that I needed to get downstairs and get my chores done. Her frustration carried a sense of disgust that quickly cloaked me as well. I felt embarrassment at her catching me in an emotional outburst that she didn't seem to understand. The incident left me feeling shattered, confused, and hollow. All I wanted was for her to hold me, rock me, and calm me.

Recalling the shame I felt, I vowed not to have emotional outbursts again. But that didn't work out because I was a sensitive child and cried easily, which only stimulated more frustration in my parents. I tried to hide my tears or stop them from flowing, as the message seemed clear that tears were not something my parents cared to see, and I detested making them angry or upset with me, or worse yet, having them be disgusted by me and my actions. To me, making adults unhappy meant that I had done something wrong.

This belief played out in another scene that came up as I let Mona's words wash over me. It was the time of my preparation for First Reconciliation, a sacrament given great ceremony in the Catholic Church. As an eight-year-old, I considered this a very special time in my life; I would go to confession and admit my sins, then I could be absolved and purified. I looked forward to being free from the guilt and shame of having sinned and took this first time of receiving the sacrament very seriously. I began to work on a list of all my sins, anything I could remember doing that was wrong. I had pages and pages of small indiscretions that showed I was, indeed, a true sinner and needed the sacrament that would make me all right in the world again.

I showed the list to my mother, thinking she would be pleased at my honesty, but instead she seemed surprised. Then she explained to me that I didn't have to list everything I had ever done that was wrong and I certainly didn't have to write it all down and take the paper into the confessional with me; just listing the bigger things would be enough for me to receive forgiveness for everything I had done. So I didn't take my list into the confessional and I stated only a few sins. But even after receiving the sacrament of Reconciliation I didn't feel that sense of cleansing I had expected. I didn't feel good enough or that it was enough for me to just be who I was. I am not sure I ever felt that way about myself.

But still, I had never even considered questioning my religion. Nor had I ever considered questioning my parents, who taught me my religion. My religion, after all, was my guidance, my way. My parents also were my teachers who knew better than I, so I would not question what they said. I questioned only myself and who I was or wasn't.

I was aware of Mona's words slowly penetrating the hard shell around me: the shell I had created to protect my upbringing and my religious beliefs and teachings; the shell I had believed to be a strong foundation, my foundation. Perhaps religion and spirituality had to be considered, as they played such predominant roles in my life. And perhaps my parents didn't have all the answers even though I hesitated to voice this thought even to myself; after all, I never questioned my parents.

As Mona's words echoed through me, filling me like liquid soaked up by a dry sponge, I shuddered. I was afraid to let myself even consider these overpowering words because they sounded like doctrine that went against every iota of what I had been taught, what I had so readily absorbed into my very being. But once Mona said, "You are the gift; there is nothing you have to do; you are already perfect; you are God," it was as if there was no going back. I began, even if only momentarily, to see myself from a different perspective, no longer a lowly sinner but a person with some qualities, something to offer the world, something to offer myself. Even the little girl in me, the one who needed to be rocked, felt some sun on her face.

Although I left my therapy session feeling more anxious and uncomfortable than when I went in, I began to have some clarity as the shell continued to disintegrate around me. At the core of it all was the belief system I had about myself, but there was nothing substantial about those beliefs. I was always changing who I must be in order to prove that I was lovable to the person I was with at the time. No wonder I didn't love myself; I didn't even know who I was. I was nothing. My shell was gone, leaving me to feel this huge void, an abyss of darkness and loneliness and nothingness. What had gone wrong?

I wondered, what would really happen if I didn't go to church on Sunday? I had gone to chapel at the hospital, but it wasn't a Catholic service. I knew you could be exempt from church on Sunday if you were sick. Surely I was sick enough to be exempt, I told myself. And what would it mean if I wasn't sick enough to be exempt? One question merely led to another. Did my parents love me, or was it what I did that they loved? Did anyone really love me? Would people love me if I started to say no to them? Was I really alone in this world? Did I even have a relationship with God?

Once the questions started, they continued, making me very aware of my aloneness. Usually if I had questions, I would just seek someone out to find an answer. But no one was here with me at the hospital. And I didn't want to even see anyone; I didn't trust their love for me. I did have Mona to help me process some of these questions, but I knew I needed to sit with myself and find the answers.

It was in that aloneness that I shifted where I looked for my answers. Ravenous for information and understanding, I began to read, seeking answers about spirituality that would validate me. I wanted to find evidence that I was already good and whole and that I could just embrace myself as I was, and I wanted to understand how to get to the love for myself. I read any self-help book or spiritual book I could find, borrowing them from my therapist, other patients, nurses, and my psychiatrist. I didn't filter what I read as I wanted to learn about perspectives—whether spiritual or psychological—that were new to me.

And as I read, more questions came up. One answer would contradict another, and there was never one to calm me down and allow me to feel full and complete. It was really the same approach I had always used, allowing something from the outside to build my inner framework.

I eventually stopped reading and started journaling. It was a foreign coping mechanism to me, but Mona had suggested I journal to begin to get in touch with myself. So I started to write, and it felt better than anything I had yet discovered. I felt like I was spending time with myself and validating my own feelings, something I certainly had never done before. The feelings poured out of my heart. It was as if I had flipped a switch and was suddenly overflowing with so much to say to myself, so much to listen to, so much to pay attention to within myself. Writing soothed me, helped me clarify what I did feel and know, made things more concrete so that I could look within myself and begin the practice of listening to myself. I always had felt so unheard that it was refreshing to know I could take care of this need on my own.

Writing also mirrored myself back to me, allowing me, maybe for the first time ever, to see a clearer picture. Little by little, feelings would come to light, feelings that I had set aside or ignored all my life, feelings about my own needs rather than others' needs. Slowly I began to see how little I paid attention to myself, how little I heard my intuition, my own knowing within.

I would write about Jerry and how he was unhappy with me for being gone so long and not getting better, and about how my parents were upset with me for being at the hospital and told me to get home. I knew I had to be here, but no one else supported it; it was a break in my pattern of always focusing on others.

As I wrote, I was able to find some self-awareness. I came to realize that being alone at this time was perfect; I needed to seek my own answers and not be swayed by those I loved, and this understanding eased the pain of feeling so alone. If people were around, I would not yet know how to block out their opinions and just listen to my own. I might just continue to take on their needs. These insights came out in my writing, often surprising me. I started to acknowledge that I had wisdom within me.

I was grateful to have found writing as it allowed me to touch my soul. And I wanted to expand this connection. I wanted to learn how to just sit and be quiet with myself and listen to what was going on inside of me, so I asked other hospital residents, therapists, and class leaders about meditation. Another patient knew how to meditate, and we began to meditate together; I learned to sit with my eyes closed, just breathing, listening to calming music, and letting the thoughts go. And although it was not physically hard to sit this way, it was a foreign experience to me. To me meditation was prayer, and my form of prayer was to ask a Being outside of myself for help, or give thanks for prayers answered, or ask for strength to be good, or beg for the Peace of God to be upon me. I didn't know how to just sit and listen, how to let things roll in or out. I didn't even know how to breathe deeply as I sat quietly. It was really uncomfortable, and from my perspective my first try was quite unsuccessful.

Still, with my shell gone, a foundation needed to be built. The pain of having my beliefs and everything I had lived for torn down was unbearable. The only thing I really knew is that I loved my children enough to put myself in this hospital and work on myself, even though it would have been easier to end the pain by ending my life. The process in the hospital was a hard time, but I would do anything for my children.

And so the questions flowed because I could no longer stop them. The pressure built within, and I became determined to use my new skills to find answers. I journaled to hear myself, tried to sit quietly and listen within, and worked on breathing to still my rambling thoughts.

Listening to my own heart was going to be a hard task. I was so impressionable that I still didn't know where I started and where others started. I didn't begin to know who I was. Being part of God was the furthest thing from my truth. But then at that time, I didn't know what my truth was or if I even had my own truths. The emptiness I felt made my feelings of being nothing only more prominent.

Chapter 16

Please Stop the Rain

As the weeks of my hospitalization continued to stretch into months, Jerry's pain grew to be insurmountable. His life had fallen apart. He had a business to run, three children to care for, and a wife in the psychiatric ward in a hospital fifty miles away. I was gone, gone in a way he had never experienced. My physical absence made life very difficult, but the reason for this absence was even tougher. He didn't know where to go for comfort and support, some relief. The extended family on both sides was starkly absent. He couldn't talk to me. He knew he had to be the strong one, and it was a struggle to even get out of bed each morning, but he had to for the kids. Even though he had no energy, someone had to be the parent, a truth he had expressed resentfully on more than one occasion.

He was bitter, but perhaps it was more fear, fear that he couldn't hold on much longer. He felt that he was going under, drowning. Doubts and questions added to a burden that felt too heavy for him to carry alone. And it scared him because it was in these moments that treading water was too much and he would feel himself sinking.

He yearned to have me back for more than just my companionship. The daily tasks—cooking, cleaning, laundry, paying the bills, doing the grocery shopping, chauffeuring the kids, helping them with homework, and getting them bathed and to bed at a decent time—were a constant barrage of reminders, like arrows reminding him of his pain. He missed my way of keeping the house running like a finely tuned engine; nothing seemed to run smoothly anymore. He didn't have the limber fingers needed to fix the girls' hair, and he often mismatched the outfits that the kids wore. At seven, Jessica knew which pieces of clothing went together, which outfits were for playing in and which outfits were for special occasions, so she would gently lead Jerry through picking out the appropriate clothing for her little sister.

It was strange how Jessica seemed to intuitively know what was happening, even though we hadn't talked about it. She helped her daddy, becoming like a second mother to the family, and though we both knew it wasn't right, he needed her. She could tell him how I did things as he attempted to keep some routine in their disrupted lives. Routine was important for all of them; it gave them some reprieve from the downpour of rain. But Jessica's stepping into this role also made his ache stronger. He knew it was his responsibility and yet he couldn't shoulder it alone. I, too, saw this small child trying to carry the weight of helping out, which added to my own guilt and shame.

Jeremy, in his own way, tried to hold down the fort by bossing his sisters around, which only caused more fighting between them, more grief that their mom wasn't there to keep the peace.

Jacqui was another story. She was four years old, the baby of the family, and quite independent—maybe a bit spoiled and perhaps missing her mommy too much. Mornings presented the first challenge for Jerry, as Jacqui couldn't stand to have her hair brushed. So the break of day was a blend of nurturing, pleading, and demanding as he sat her down to get her hair combed before she was taken to the babysitter. If he brushed too fast or caught an unseen tangle, she would release a blood-curdling scream and tears would flow instantly as she raced around the living room in a circle. Her scream would become silent as she lost her breath. Then the real drama began; she would panic because she couldn't breathe. Jumping up and down in an attempt to communicate her crisis only caused more chaos, and it then took more time to get her settled down and cajoled into letting him try again.

He tried to maintain the family standards: the children had always been clean, well dressed, and well groomed. But no matter what he did, the girls' hair never looked like it did when I fixed it. When the kids came to visit me, the girls would often have hair in their eyes. Tangles were hidden under the first layer, and their hair had lost its lustrous glow. I just had to do something about it, and sometimes during visits we would work on their hair.

Maybe Jerry was okay with my seeing that; it was a resentful reminder that I wasn't home like I was supposed to be for these little but important daily tasks. He was right. I had left him to take care of the children, and so I should be satisfied with how he was doing it. The kids were confused about my absence, and the hair issue seemed to be symbolic of many details in their lives that were being ignored or neglected. They all needed some time and attention from me; they needed me, and their outer appearance mirrored the inner turmoil they obviously each felt.

During the day, the kids often played with their friends in the neighborhood, which allowed them some time to get away from the reminders of home. Perhaps this was how they managed the sea of pain that they were thrust into once they arrived back home for the evening.

Evenings were hardest for everyone. The kids would often end up in Jerry's bed after waking up from nightmares. This offered them some comfort from their worries about when and if I was coming back home and whether Jerry was going to leave too, a concern they silently brooded about.

Every so often Jerry would verbalize his feelings over whether it had been right to check me in to the hospital. Usually it was a mix of anger, resentment, and confusion, which always made me feel worse than I already felt. But in a weak moment a few weeks after I was admitted, he shared some understanding of my plight.

The day after he checked me in, he had been driving to work and was delayed by a funeral. As he pulled over and watched the procession drive by and into the cemetery, he understood the severity of my situation. He had heard about this death; the funeral was for a young woman close to my age who had committed suicide that week. The feelings it gave him were strangely surreal; he knew that he could have been burying me and felt he had been given a sign that it was right for me to be at the hospital.

He would sometimes recall this reminder that there could have been a chilling permanent outcome for our family. In those moments he realized he was breathing with relief that I was safe. Still another part of him felt as if I had died and been buried, almost as if I had made the choice to leave him by pulling the trigger on that horrible night. He felt abandoned, unloved, uncared for, and terribly alone. He tried to focus on my choice to go to the hospital as a positive one, but the feelings still played out strongly and he ached with the deep wound my absence inflicted upon him.

Although it was hard to hear this outpouring from Jerry, I knew I needed to practice letting it go and leaving him to deal with his own feelings. This was part of my problem: I always took care of others even at the cost of my own well-being, but not stepping in now was easier because I had no energy to do anything. It was probably this new pattern of mine that only deepened Jerry's sense of abandonment. We were each other's best friends and if I had physically left him and was shutting him out emotionally, he couldn't help but feel a heavy sense of betrayal.

Often after Jerry had the children in bed, the quiet of the house echoed too strongly, and he would sit down to play the piano. The piano was home to him. As his fingers stroked the keys, he could express himself. One particular evening his pain was so intense that it burst through in song. As the notes became alive with the strength and force of the pain, the words began to tumble out of his mouth in the form of a desperate prayer.

> I ask for just a moment
> To tell you how I feel.
> It seems so hard to touch you.
> How much of this is real?
>
> I think I must be dreaming,
> And things will be all right.
> Please look into my eyes, sweet love,
> And let me hold you tight.

For I love you,
My body holds my pain.
I just want to hold you.
My God, please stop the rain.

To love me is to trust me.
My feelings are so true.
I'm not something that I can't be,
I am I and you are you.

For I love you,
My body holds my pain.
I just want to hold you.
My God, please stop the rain.

He broke down and sobbed. My breakdown was the breakdown of our entire family—its structure, its functioning, and our lives together. It was gone, washed away. And with this great loss came a deep sense of grief, a sadness and confusion that affected each of us. The children were too young to have developed the emotional skills to stay afloat, but there they were, floundering, trying to swim, going under frequently, and holding on for dear life to whatever support they found. Jerry had always used me for emotional support and I was gone. Each had to carry on alone, and there was nothing to stop the rain. There was no moment to rest.

Jerry watched for the kids as they bobbed in the sea of sorrow, and with what little strength he had left he would take them on his shoulders, but it wasn't long before he had to ask them to carry their own load for a while. They didn't seem to have a place to rest their weary souls. Home as they knew it was gone. The rain had washed home away, that familiar solace, even that familiar smell of home that allows us to rest and relax in its comforts. It was gone, lost. "My God," he thought, "I hope I can hold on."

And while Jerry played his song and we all treaded the stormy waters, these lyrics burst forth from me:

Hey world, here I am!
Isn't anyone glad to see me?
I've arrived!
Where have you each gone?
No, I have released the old me—
But I'm here
Do you want to know me?

I feel
alone
with this—
Somehow the support is not there
For me to feel free . . .
But world,
I do—
I may have to rejoice
Alone
But my burden has lightened
I can fly now
I can see,
Feel,
Hear,
Love now . . .
I can't go back to sleep

So my task at hand
Must be
To
Muster the strength
To
Stand alone
In
Me.

Chapter 17

Gratitude

A small bird zipped by almost as if to signal me. The movement brought me back to the hill—back to the present—as dusk was settling in. As I got cozy for the night, I practiced deep breathing. Done properly, with deep breaths drawn into the abdomen, it helped me stay more aware of the present moment rather than reflecting on the past. It was a skill I had worked hard to master, and I often reminded myself not to take it for granted.

As I lay in my sleeping bag watching the trees, aware that I was the foreigner here in the midst of nature, gratitude flooded over me. The five trees in front of me, to the west, continued to give me a sense of calm. The side pine trees, my pine trees, stood guard as if to protect me, and gave me a sense of belonging. All the trees seemed to be opening their arms to me, embracing me. Trees had become more and more my friends. I was aware of their energy and their gift of sharing themselves with me: their protection, their shade, their beauty.

As night set in, I became more conscious that the minor headache I had was becoming much worse. Once more, I breathed deeply. I made prayers to the four directions before retreating for the evening. I made a prayer for my headache to go away. Locusts were out, singing very loudly, and I could hear several crows in the distance. Their cawing seemed to vibrate in my head, making my headache even more painful. The trees began to quiet for the night, without the rustling of their leaves or the bending of their branches in the wind. In their stillness I sensed compassion and felt protected. Above me the mosquitoes were swarming, but they did not seem to notice me.

As night settled in, I felt the dew beginning to form on my sleeping bag. I recalled how, before my hospitalization, I had always been afraid of being alone at night; I would never have willingly been out on a hill by myself in the black of night. Not only would the darkness have been a threat but the creatures that lurked beyond the hill would also have become a dire terror in my head. But with no fear tonight I could take pleasure in how comfortable and safe I felt. The distant evening sounds were a lullaby that relaxed me in preparation for sleep.

Down below, my supporters were in a different world. The wind howled, bending the trees in an intense crescendo, and it blew through the camp with a vengeance. Taking turns to tend the fire throughout the night, they found little comfort in its warmth. The fire, representing the light and consciousness that burns within us, had been started before I went out on the hill and was to burn until I returned to camp. Symbolically, the sacred fire was to support me on the hill as I faced myself, burning away all that was false so that I might see the truth. While my friends stood at the fire, chilled to the bone, they made prayers for me to be given the journey I was meant to have during this vision quest. They also prayed that I was keeping warm this cold, windy night.

Lying in my sleeping bag and looking up at the stars, I watched a magnificent light show. The clearness of the night sky allowed deep layers of stars to show themselves in a way I had never before witnessed. This spectacle seemed fitting of a vision quest that was to guide me to see deep beyond my surface. Appreciating each point of splendor in the sky, I sought to appreciate the beauty within myself.

At one point I felt a calling from a star that stood out among the rest, encouraging me to crane my neck toward the south flag. Turning over onto my stomach, I was able to fully take in the bright star. At first it appeared to have movement, and I thought it might be an airplane. But as I studied it I realized it was a star, and I was awed by its intensity. I whispered a prayer of gratitude to it for reminding me to pay attention to all the small details that were so magnificent in the backdrop of life, then turned back over to watch the quickly moving cloud formations.

Where had the clouds come from? I wondered. I saw formations shifting until they fit together as if they were forming a Lakota star to fill the sky. It took my breath away as I recalled the vision I had had months ago: the Lakota star that had covered my ceiling as I lay in bed. And once again I witnessed an opening in the center that called me into it, like an invitation to enter and fully see the glory of who I was. I felt the magical moment once again, the validation that all was in order. And with that validation came a deep sense of peace within. I couldn't help but remember my search, my yearning, my unending drive to find that inner peace. Now here I lay, by myself in the midst of nature, just me, my soul, and God—the Universe. I felt full, oh so full.

But even in my peace, I was aware of my aching head, which seemed to become worse as the evening wore on. Eventually sitting up was my only recourse; the pain from the pressure of lying down was too much to tolerate. Sitting up, I did some deep breathing, trying to release the headache. I searched within myself to pay attention to what else I needed to release; what was I holding on to with such resistance that it would give me a headache? A locust continued to sing loudly, feeling to me as if it lived in my head. There were crickets in the distance, and once in a while I would notice a frog croaking. But in spite of my pain, the night remained still, the stars remained bright, the dark never receded into blackness, and I remained content. Excruciatingly aware of every sound, I could not sleep, so I paid attention. The night cradled me.

My headache and the sense of the earth caring for me made me recall a time when a bad headache had led me to feeling nurtured and joyous. This awful headache brought Jerry, my first and only love, into my life. I was just fourteen and waiting tables at the Kopper Kettle, a restaurant just a few miles from my home. Jerry and I had worked the same shifts for a few weeks, but he was a gas station attendant and I was waitressing in the adjoining restaurant, so I hadn't even noticed him. But that changed after our first encounter. Twenty-four years later it was still vivid in my mind.

On a particularly busy day, I ventured out into the gift shop to see if there was any aspirin for a headache that was starting to get in the way of my work. A handsome young man was standing behind the counter with the cashier, Ronda. Walking toward them, I felt his eyes on me, but didn't have time to consider meeting him as I had a full section in the restaurant to keep me on task. Asking Ronda if she had any aspirin, I glanced over at the attractive dark-haired man, who appeared about a year or two older than I. Our gazes met, and I quickly found myself locked and lost in his warm, vivid sea-blue eyes. I was caught off guard by my inability to draw my eyes away, and my heart pounded. He reached up and touched my forehead with his palm, sending tingling through my body, then rummaged through the top drawer just under the cash register until he found the aspirin. He handed two to me and I took them as I made my way back to the restaurant to attend to my tables.

I went home different that night. His kindness and compassion—foreign but so inviting—had taken me by surprise, and I yearned for more. A month later, Jerry and I started dating. Certainly life sometimes brings pain in to guide us where we least expect it.

My pounding head brought me back to the hill. The air was fresh and as I worked to inhale deeply I felt cleansed, despite my headache. Perhaps this pain would also lead me to a deeper healing or bring joy into my life. I certainly knew from my hospitalization experience that pain-ridden journeys could lead to wellness.

Down below, my supporters had their own focus. Although one always remained to tend the fire, the rest were nursing Vicki because she had the most horrible headache she had ever experienced. Beginning to consider whether she would need medical attention, the group set out to care for her.

One of the supporters gave her water therapy, placing water on her forehead and allowing it to cool her. Another offered her healing touch therapy. As the evening moved into night, her pain receded slightly. But she was not able to lie down—just as I, on the hill, was not able to lie down and sleep—so she stayed awake watching the stars, listening to the howling wind, and trying to stay warm. She, too, knew that the headache symbolized a need for release and openness. She contemplated what this meant for her individually and for the supporters as a group, and made prayers for guidance in releasing whatever she might be holding on to.

Early in the dawn, I finally slept and after several hours awoke to a drumbeat echoing through the canyon, letting me know that my supporters were making prayers for me. The drum sang to me for a long time, and during its serenade an owl hooted off to the north. As I stretched and greeted the morning I caught sight of movement below: three white-tailed deer were romping and snorting, playing together as the sun rose. The drumbeat synchronized with my heartbeat, and nature seemed in unison with both. I felt connected.

As the sun quietly entered my day, I too rose, folding my bedding and looking forward to a glorious day. Just the mere fact that the sun was shining was a gift since we had been hammered with hurricane rains in the days preceding my vision quest. My heart swelled as I shifted into a state of appreciation and grace. The loving prayers of those down below, the warming sun, the joyful animals, and the overall beauty and calm surrounding me gave me such an awareness of the love I so longed for. I was aware of the completeness I felt, the contentment, the peace that brought more gratitude since I had searched all my life for such peace. Finally here it was, deep within myself.

I sat with these feelings, allowing them to immerse me just as my surroundings did—the rolling hills, the sunlit meadows, and the gently swaying trees. I focused on the gratitude I felt within my heart and let it embrace my entire body. Taking off my shoes, I let the grass caress my feet. The sun began to beat down, bringing beads of sweat to my forehead, and I covered my head with my sunbonnet. As I sat at each corner meditating and watching the land, I prayed to the Spirits of the four directions.

Later, I stood and held my pipe upward and spontaneously made a prayer to Father Sky for Mona, my therapist, who had known how to help me heal ten years ago. The prayer surprised me because I hadn't been thinking of Mona. But as I prayed, I began to cry. I was puzzled by this deep emotion but allowed myself to feel the sorrow, and then the release that welled up with my tears. Feeling as if I had been holding the pain back, I lay on the ground and let myself empty out like a vessel.

As I rested, lyrics started to come to me and eventually I felt a need to sing. I had never been much of a singer, so I resisted the urge. But I knew I had to let the song out. And although it was not beautifully sung, it held a certain loveliness that touched my soul when I heard the words vibrating in the sky.

> Peace, my child, I love you so.
> Peace, my child, I love you so.
> Peace, my child, I love you so,
> Unconditionally.

These words seemed to come from above, from the Great Spirit to me. As I took in the message, my tears turned to intense sobs that reached into a profound place within me. As I touched this place deep inside, there was a melting within and I felt an emotional release, a relief brought by my tears. Although the expression was one of deep, deep sadness, there was also deep joy. The sadness came from memories of feeling unlovable and lonely: feelings that I had throughout most of my growing-up years, feelings that were being stirred deeply at this moment. And the joy was from the immense love that permeated my being when these song lyrics came forth. It felt like someone very dear to me was telling me there was a true love for me. I felt it deep within my heart.

Still on the ground, I allowed my body to quiet itself as a calm came over me. The song continued to flow through my head, and I recalled Mona coming into my life. She had been the person telling me, "Peace, my child, I love you so." She had reflected my lovability.

There had been that deep sadness, so profound that I had checked myself in to the hospital. Mona was the sweet part of that bitter experience. She had created the space to allow expression of the pain. She had held me as I cried nonstop for months. She had loved me unconditionally, which was the catalyst in my healing. She had taught me to feel. In some ways it all seemed like yesterday, and in some ways it seemed like another lifetime.

So much had changed after I came home. I had changed. Of course it had been natural, even after ten years, that I would lift my pipe to say a prayer of gratitude for Mona; she had saved my life while teaching me how to live life more fully. Because of her I could sit here on the hill, taking in the splendid beauty that surrounded me. And because of her, I had found peace right here, within me.

Chapter 18

Breathing

After four months at the hospital, I came home. I felt like a baby chick that had pecked its way out of the egg, but was still wet, fragile, and struggling to learn how to live in this world. I wanted do more than to survive; I wanted to thrive. Leaving the hospital meant leaving my support, the people who had helped me listen to myself and encouraged me to try new ways. Going home meant I had to confront the debris that had always stood in my way, as well as my family's expectation that things would return to normal when I came back. Things were never back to "normal" again.

Nor could I let life go back to the way it had been. I knew my breakdown had been my soul stopping me dead in my tracks, calling for me to pay attention. I had hit a brick wall and it tumbled down on me. My soul had given me other signs, gentler signs, but after years of ignoring myself a jolting experience was the only way I was finally able to listen to my soul's calling. The pain of being disconnected from myself had been insurmountable, and I had no desire to ever go back to that time.

So life as we knew it had to change. We started by closing doors that no longer served us in order to open new ones. Jerry decided to leave the family business to pursue a career in law enforcement. His decision meant that the business was put up for sale. My father was angry with us and made this clear when he took our shares in the business, but Jerry told him that he needed his sanity.

Several months later, he was hired as a police officer. This meant a change in his schedule—he started out working the night shift—and a substantial drop in our income. Until the details of hiring a new manager could be settled, he was still working in the business, so he was carrying two jobs. But all of this seemed to not matter as much as doing what we needed to do, what was right for us.

Because I had been so moved by the process of what therapy had done for me, I closed my drapery business and started a six-year program to become a clinical social worker. I had never attended college, and I realized that developing myself was part of my healing process.

At first, Jerry had not been happy about my decision. In fact, he said that if I went to school he would divorce me. I understood that I was throwing a monkey wrench into our routine. He had married me with the idea that I would stay home with the children and take care of our household. I assured him that I understood his position, and I accepted the possibility that he might not want to stay with me if I went forward with my plans. But ultimately, I had to do what would heal me and he would have to do the same. I worked to accept that I couldn't control his choices, his reactions, but only my choices and reactions. I refused to become fearful of his threat to leave me; instead I focused on remembering that it would all work out one way or the other. I had given him full permission to leave me. Accepting the reality that I had no control over Jerry's choices was significant, as was my decision to move forward in spite of his disapproval.

Attending college meant I would not be home every day with the children; nor would I be able to do all the domestic chores that I once had managed. Our patterns had to change, with each person contributing to the family's needs. One night, after a terrible argument about who needed to cook dinner, Jerry and I took a pad and pen and went to have coffee at Country Kitchen. Writing down everything that absolutely had to be done each week in the home, we split the tasks I had held previously, and gave each of us specific cooking nights. Jerry was willing to give it a try since we both wanted our home to be calmer and to run more efficiently.

The kids had to assume more responsibility for their individual needs. They brought down their own clothing to be laundered, folded it and put it away, cleaned their rooms, made their beds, and also had to contribute more to the household tasks. We cleaned house together on Saturdays; five of us could get it done in a third of the time it would take me to do it alone. Everyone helped clean up the dishes after dinner, which changed a forty-five-minute job into a ten-minute task.

College was new for me and certainly another stretch in my development. Because I craved the structure to learn and expand my knowledge base, and learning came easy for me, I realized that I had not been living up to my full potential. I had needed to walk forward in this educational journey. It was scary, but I loved it once I became acclimated to my professors' expectations.

I took an Eastern Psychology class in my second semester. In this class we practiced meditation in a dojo, which gave me scheduled time to practice sitting with myself and breathing appropriately: in through my nose until my abdomen expanded, then out through my mouth. I had always been a stressed person and tended to breathe shallowly, causing more anxiousness.

What I learned about breathing in that course helped me realize how important it was for my continued growth and healing. Improper breathing can be a common cause of illnesses because it causes depletion in the immune system and increases stress levels. Proper breathing supports calmness, by allowing the body to take in the oxygen it needs, giving its cells energy to operate in a functional manner.

I started going to the dojo twice a week and participated in an early morning meditation before my first class. We would sit cross-legged, facing a wall, with our eyes open but looking downward. We would remain in this position for the entire fifty minutes of meditation. My focus was on my breath. I worked to take it into my belly, following it down with my mind's eye, and then back up to exhale. I would imagine myself facing the ocean, breathing in the salt air as the waves washed over me. Exhaling, I imagined myself as a grain of sand, riding out with a wave until I disappeared into the endless ocean. I practiced this breathing technique as I sat quietly with myself for many months, and long after that semester I continued to go to the dojo.

Through meditation, I also learned to quiet down the outer noise, which allowed me to hear my inner world much better. It was in these quiet times that I could hear Mona's voice in my head, reminding me of what I had learned in the hospital or telling me to slow down, set boundaries, and not be everything to everyone. It was during these quiet times that I could access her love for me, her holding of me, which helped me soothe myself during difficult moments. It was during these times that I could assess how I had handled something and consider whether it had been the right way for me. Spending time with myself, I slowly started to find energy and passion in living fully each day. Each day grew more beautiful as I listened to myself and used my new skills to see and live life differently.

Jerry's decision to change careers and get out of the family business made my father unhappy and angry with us. His reaction was unbalancing to both Jerry and me. Our marriage was on rather shaky ground as we tried to find a new way to be with each other. Our children were struggling because the mom they once knew was not the same mom who came home. At one point Jeremy, then ten, stood in the middle of our living room during one of our family meetings and, with tears running down his cheeks, he cried out, "I know it's good for you to go to school and I don't want you to quit, but it's so hard to be independent, Mom. I miss you fixing the supper and sewing all the time." He spoke for the family with his next words: "What about next summer?" The summer I had been gone had been a long, difficult one, and when I came home, life was supposed to get back to normal.

So with Jeremy's words resonating with each of us, we continued forward. Yes, it would have been easier to go back to the way life had always been. But I knew it wasn't right and so we fought onward. When I could, I stood strong in my new patterns and tried to make the best of each day as it came our way.

The new structure in the home did help to give the kids clarity in the expectations, and the rhythm of the new ways began to happen. But the issues with the family business, our marriage, my schooling, and Jerry's new job brought up a constant barrage of challenges. With our footing not solidified, this often caused emotional difficulties. But we remained consistent in coming back to the structure and maintaining baby steps through the debris.

It had been a very painful time in our family leading up to the hospitalization. I had been unhappy and that unhappiness caused chaos in the family. Of course, during my hospitalization, my absence caused my family great grief. But it was after the hospitalization when the real work began. Life was never the same after I came home; we had to find a new rhythm, a new family dance step and a new marital dance. It was grueling. It broke my heart to see my children in such turmoil, such pain. It confused them that I was gone several days per week at school, when all of their lives I had been a "stay-at-home" mom. Even though I worked in our two businesses, I always had the flexibility to be home with the children and I scheduled my day in that way.

Jerry wasn't happy that I was going to school, but I was unwavering in my decision. I wasn't thrilled that he had chosen to change careers at this time, as our income had gone down. Yet there was a core part of each of us that knew we had to respect each other in these significant changes. We both knew there were no guarantees we would make the transitions as a couple, and we also knew we couldn't compromise ourselves in an effort to make the marriage work, so this was very new ground for us.

Through all of this, there were times we stumbled, not knowing exactly how to make life better. The journey of our recovery was a slow process. In the end I wouldn't have done it differently. I had found so much of myself in the process. How could I wish that to be different? And even though my family had experienced such profound pain, I had to do the work to allow myself to finally break open my shell and venture out into the world. Without it, I was nothing for myself or for them.

I had continued to practice being strong in myself, learning how to be quiet, sit with myself, and just breathe. No matter how long I practiced, it never came easy, but it did come. As deep breathing became more natural, I noticed decisions came easier because I could more quickly decipher what was right for me. The new information that I was learning in college opened exciting new avenues for me in how I thought about everything and what I wanted out of life. Jerry was experiencing the same in his new career as a policeman. The family became more comfortable in the new ways of operating, and Jerry and I learned to talk more and listen to each other better. Eventually the peace that I sought began to find me.

Chapter 19

Embraced

I cried and I slept. When I awoke, I stood and once again raised my pipe toward the sky. I prayed out loud in the wilderness to the Great Spirit for others—my husband, my children, and my parents. As I did, more lyrics came to me, bringing an inner pressure that needed release. I stopped praying for others and focused on the message that was coming to me.

The words to the song continued to develop, and as I heard them inside myself, they touched me deeply. My tears flowed; I felt so genuinely loved with an authenticity that also brought up all the times I had felt unloved and unlovable. The lyrics and the melody instilled in me a warmth that embraced me fully for who I was in this moment. Where were the lyrics and the melody coming from? I wasn't a musical person and I could hardly keep a tune. But the song continued and I felt this sense of purging as I sang whatever needed to be expressed.

> I am Mother Earth beneath.
> Hear my heart beat one with you.
> Let me hold and rock you now.

Let me cuddle close to you.
Let me wrap you tightly
In this blanket, warmly.
Lay your head upon my breast
As my arms caress you.
Let me hold you, rock and sing,
As I love you so.

Peace, my child, I love you so.
Peace, my child, I love you so.
Peace, my child, I love you so,
Unconditionally.

Alone, I sang the song out loud and allowed the melody to reverberate throughout the hills. I practiced over and over, afraid I would forget the tune. And the more I sang the lyrics, the more deeply they touched me.

Drugged with overwhelming feelings, I slept on and off all day. My body limp with heaviness, I fell deeply into Mother Earth's caress, her lyrics echoing in my unconscious as her love moved through my veins. In my waking moments, I struggled for my normal daytime clarity. I stood with my face upward, hoping that the sun would dissipate the fog I experienced. I felt somewhere between dreaming and wakefulness, and I wondered what was really happening to me. Were these lyrics coming to me in a dream state?

The day passed as I slept, awoke, sang the words that poured forth, cried more tears, and then fell into another deep sleep. The song continued to develop, as if the universe were giving me a message to soothe me, reassure me, and remind me that I was loved and cared for, that I was really never alone. New lyrics came.

I am Father Sky above.
See my arms stretched way beyond.
Let me reach down, pick you up,
Bring you near as my arms close.
Let me wrap you tightly
In this blanket, warmly.
Lay your head upon my breast.
Hear my heart beat one with you.
Let me hold and rock you now.
Let me sing and cuddle close.

Peace, our child, we love you so.
Peace, our child, we love you so.
Peace, our child, we love you so,
Unconditionally.

As the song progressed from "my child" to "our child," from "I" to "we," I once again felt loved and understood. Mother Earth, representing the nurturing of a mother holding her child, and Father Sky, representing the protectiveness of a father, were allowing me to feel safe in the world, in a way I had always yearned for.

And with this experience on the hill came a deep awareness that I could always feel this way. I was surrounded with protection and nurturing. I had only to notice it, realize it was there, and awaken it within myself. It was the answer to my life question, my continual searching, and the answer was found within me—felt there—deeply. Emptied and drained, I fought to understand the full meaning of all that had manifested that day.

With the onset of dusk, I prepared for the storm that I knew would probably be coming because this was a vision quest and that seemed to be the way these things went. I certainly wanted my altar relics to stay dry, so I tucked them into their plastic bag. Once again, I spread the tarp, laid my sleeping bag out over it, and tucked my two quilts into my sleeping bag. I added thermal underwear to my attire and crawled into the sleeping bag, settling in for the night. I loved the crisp night air that seemed to bathe me, which was one of the gifts of sleeping outside that had always appealed to me. Life felt so good.

As night moved in, I fell into a deep sleep that seemed to take me elsewhere. Sometime in the night, I dreamed that a mother cat came to visit me. She was pure white and bigger than a lion, with large paws that looked soft. Her fur, which hung on her with wrinkles, was inviting as she allowed me to lie next to her. As we lay there, I studied her, knowing she had come to teach me something.

Large Mother Cat was my animal totem, and her appearing to me in a dream was significant. She was the mother of all big cats, and she stated that she had come to me in my dream state to remind me that she walked with me and would teach me how to access the gifts I had to offer the world. It was another affirmation that I was never really alone, that guidance and support came in many ways to me as I walked the Red Road, the path of integrity in life. I dreamed through the night and slept soundly, without the rainstorm I had expected, which I considered another gift from the universe.

Dawn, however, arrived to greet me with cold rain on my face. I sighed, relieved that I would not have to experience a storm in the night while I was on the hill. Today was my final day. The cold droplets seemed like a small cross to bear and I gave gratitude for the daytime rain. I checked the pipe I had brought and the envelope carrying my father's message and feather. Finding them safe, I nestled back into my sleeping bag and pulled the tarp up and over my head. Cocooned and dry, I cuddled with the quilts as I listened to the pat, pat, pat of the drops hitting the tarp. Utter contentment came from the feelings of warmth and safety. Every part of my body soaked it in, and a new feeling of wholeness embraced me.

My body curled into the ground as if a place had been carved out for me. I inhaled the smell of the earth, the soft dirt that held my body. Lyrics from the day before rang through my head as I lay still, conscious of my heart beating, allowing it to sink into synchronicity with Mother Earth. Yes, I felt she was present, holding me, keeping me close, rocking me gently as if I were a newborn baby. I knew I was being taken care of, being healed of that void from my early life, and I felt an overwhelming sense of love flood through my body.

And with the feelings of contentment and love came the need to sing once more. "Peace, my child, I love you so" rang throughout the hills; the words seemed to take on a life of their own, and I had no choice but to sing the lyrics out loud.

The words brought me an image of Mother Earth holding me. The message was clear, and I accepted it: I was loved, loved unconditionally, with nothing more to give but myself. I knew that even though the song came from my mouth, the words and the melody had been sent from above.

The rain droned on like the solid beat of a drum, steady and strong without a pause, as the song continued to echo in my head. It played over and over as if it needed to reach deep into my bones.

Peace, our child, we love you so.
Peace, our child, we love you so.
Peace, our child, we love you so,
Unconditionally.

The weather seemed to become wintry as the hours crept by, the wind bringing in a gusty cold. Perhaps that hurricane rain had saved itself for this day. The skies were gray, and a haze settled over me. The cold made it harder to feel the warmth from the song, and I was reminded that for some people the warmth in life was masked by the gray rain of circumstances. Perhaps in the day-to-day difficulty of surviving, parents didn't give their little ones what they really needed: nurturing, emotional connecting, and love. I thought of my own parents in their need to support their six children, their need to survive the load of life, and I knew that the warmth had potential to be there, but my parents just hadn't known how to surface it in the midst of the endless gray rain.

I worked to find the warmth again, the warmth from the song, the warmth from Mother Earth, the warmth in my heart. But I was cold from the rain and couldn't access it.

Time ticked on slowly. I didn't know how long I had been in my cocoon. And with the passage of time, the rain changed. Ever so slightly, it began to turn icy, almost forming sleet. It was just enough to peck at me with a sharp bite. My blood seemed to be moving slowly through my body, and I began to shiver. I was no longer so comfortable on the ground; it felt harder, not embracing like before, and very cold. I lay there, aching, trying to absorb the heat in my sleeping bag by not moving.

And like the rain, the song persisted.

> Tell the children of the world,
> Tell the little ones,
> Tell them they are loved so much,
> Tell them there is hope.

Suddenly the song had gone from speaking to me to speaking to all children. With this verse, my tears resumed as I felt the sadness and coldness of the world and how difficult it can be to survive and be whole. I knew only too well how important it was to know that you were loved. I felt an overpowering need to cry for these children—whoever and wherever they were. I wasn't sure that there was hope, but I sang the words anyway: "Tell them there is hope." These words didn't echo over the hills as they had yesterday. Today I was curled up in my sleeping bag, with my head covered for shelter from the rain. The words echoed softly in my sleeping bag almost as if they had fallen on deaf ears, the deaf ears of the world. Yet there were more lyrics, more information for the children.

> Teach the children of the world,
> Teach the little ones,
> Teach them they are loved so much,
> Teach them there is hope.

The lyrics had my attention. I counseled children in my private practice. I worked with children who had no hope, felt no love, knew no protection, and felt abandoned. These were troubled children. These were children who had seen the worst and managed to survive. The sadness I had seen in these children overwhelmed me as the lyrics came forth. I had to wonder how one could heal their wounded hearts.

The rain had increased in intensity, muting the muffled sobs that came from my sleeping bag. Now unheard by the wilderness, I too felt abandoned by Mother Earth and Father Sky.

And in that feeling, I wondered if pain always had to be the precursor to joy. I recalled my own journey, which had been steeped in pain before I found joy. The vision quest was following this same pattern. I was now experiencing feelings of loneliness and abandonment; what did I need to express to be released from this pain?

I had been through enough pain during my hospitalization to understand that I wanted to move through it and come out in the light on the other side. I didn't want to resist this process, but to be with it fully. And with this understanding, I continued to allow myself the grace of fully feeling what came up.

As I lay there, I realized I was wet. Rain had seeped through the tarp that was supposed to protect my sleeping bag. I must not have correctly wrapped myself up in it as the Medicine Woman had shown me. I remained still, hoping to ward off any additional leaks, but the wet area continued to spread, eventually chilling my whole body. There was no telling what time it was; with no break in the rain and or wind, the sky had been the same all day— gray. It could be hours before dusk, when the Medicine Woman would come to get me. But my mind was working to remember that this path was the way through the pain and that eventually I would be dry again. I started to hum my favorite part of the song as the words sang in my head and heart.

Peace, our child, we love you so.
Peace, our child, we love you so.
Peace, our child, we love you so,
Unconditionally.

And although I couldn't feel any warmth, the words did soothe me. But it was not a complete soothing, as the next words that came seemed to prod me into singing them, almost as if they were a prayer for the children of the world and needed to be expressed at this very moment.

Tell the children of the world,
Tell the little ones,
Tell them they are loved so much,
Tell them there is hope.

And with that I fell into sleep. The lyrics and the melody played in the background as if keeping time with the rain—and also keeping me from a restfully deep sleep in which I might have escaped some of the cold.

Chapter 20

All Alone

The cold continued to chill my body, penetrating my bones down into my soul. The song was gone; the feeling of being embraced, loved, and cared for had slowly drifted away in the dampness. I still knew the lyrics, but I didn't feel them as I had before. The void sent shivers down my body and brought on a new round of sobbing. So chilled. So cold. So alone. A fleeting thought moved through my mind: the Medicine Woman had forgotten me, forgotten to come and take me off the hill. Fear began to set in for the first time.

As I cried, there were moments when I thought the lyrics would still sing in my head. The words would start out as if in slow motion, but soon quiet would take over. I couldn't recall the melody. There was nothing.

The drenched sleeping bag soon bled into my clothes, my socks, and my quilts. I found that if I didn't move, the chill was not as bad. But if I moved any part of my body, I would shake profusely. Even when my body stopped shaking, I still felt as if my bones were quivering. I realized that I would never be able to get back to camp on my own.

My sobs continued, deep, long, and hard. Abandoned, I yearned for someone to hold me. But no one came. I held my stomach, trying to roll up in a ball to protect myself from the vicious outside world.

As I lay curled up, a vision of a baby in the fetal position flashed in front of me. This baby, lying in a crib, is crying. The room is crisp, sterile, smelling of Clorox or antiseptic, and starkly empty with the exception of monitors that surround the crib. Tape holds the mechanisms in place on her body to connect her to the monitors; an IV needle is inserted in her foot. The cries . . . the intensity of her cries tells the world of her fear and discomfort. But even with her cries, no one comes to take care of her.

She was vaguely familiar to me. I gasped as I watched my body, curled like a fetus in my sleeping bag, merge with the infant in the hospital crib. I became this baby.

I am this baby. I am in a hospital. I wail. I want someone to come and take care of me. Finally, consumed with loneliness and pain, I lie there, in the crib, exhausted, defeated. Abandoned. Unloved. The stark walls are like the gray skies, offering no marker of time.

Another wave of weeping hit me again, me as the adult, me as the baby. And as the screen flashed from one hospital stay to the next, and the baby moved through her first year of life, I felt the emotion moving through me, purging my body of memories that had no narrative, feelings that had no name, hidden in my cells, my muscles, my flesh, my entire being. My insides twisted as these feelings were torn from me, carried out in a tide of tears.

I had heard the story of my being hospitalized many times in my first year of life due to digestive issues. Now I truly knew the story.

Exhausted, I lay in the cold, wet sleeping bag. And although I was still unable to move for fear the chill would take over, I knew now that I would make it through this time on the hill.

Something very significant had happened. Receiving the vision and being back in that infantile time allowed my past to click into place. More tears flowed as I allowed myself to take it all in: the experience, the understanding, the cleansing of old cellular memories.

My heart filled with sorrow as my thoughts wandered to my own children. I hoped they had never felt this kind of pain and always knew that they had two loving parents to hold them. I hoped they knew this even when I was apart from them for the four months I was hospitalized. I had never meant to hurt them, but life circumstances had guided the inevitable. And I knew that my own parents wanted me to realize that they, too, loved me, even when I was left alone at the hospital so many times as an infant. My parents didn't understand that during the first three years of life, children develop their ability to trust others and attach securely in relationships; they didn't realize that the infant me needed them. Equally, I didn't know when I left my children for four months that it would have profound impact on their early development. I did know, however, that I loved them and did the best I knew how to do. And I also knew that my parents loved me as best they could and did the best they knew how to do. I had gone full circle from being the baby, to being the adult, to being the parent with my own babies.

I couldn't help but think of all the children I had counseled; they hadn't always been as blessed as my own children were or as I was as a child. I had met so many children without someone who cared for them, and I knew there were countless more I couldn't help.

The melody started to play in my head as I recalled the verses of Mother Earth holding me, Father Sky holding me, and then the verses about the children.

> Tell the children of the world,
> Tell the little ones,
> Tell them they are loved so much,
> Tell them there is hope.

> Teach the children of the world,
> Teach the little ones,
> Teach them they are loved so much,
> Teach them there is hope.

The next verse then came:

> Hold the children close to you.
> Wrap your arms around them.
> Rock and sing and hold them close.
> Hold them in your arms.

As I reflected upon these new lyrics, Mona, my therapist, flashed before me. She was holding me as my tears flowed. She had her arms wrapped around me, as she held me, touched me, caressed me. I wasn't alone. I needed her to touch me, hold me, nurture me. I needed someone to do it.

Children flashed through my mind, troubled children who had become my work as a counselor. My life work, my soul work: It was about holding the children—holding their souls, teaching others to hold and be there for them, helping them learn how to feel, helping them learn how to trust the world, and helping them heal. It was about helping others, even as adults, heal their childhood wounds.

I lay there listening to the patter of the rain as it hit my tarp. I knew that the Medicine Woman would not come to get me until my lessons for this vision quest were complete. Tired and empty of everything, I fell into a dreamlike state.

I found myself walking along a glowing path; it was luminous as if it were made of actual gold nuggets, and lined by trees whose fall leaves were almost iridescent in the setting sun. Vibrant tones of gold, green, red, and yellow radiated with an intensity that made me feel happy.

A child walked on each side of me; I held their hands. Behind us were more children, all led by adults holding their hands. There were thousands of children, each smiling from ear to ear, happy to be part of the group. I could hear giggling and singing as I led them further along the golden path. We followed it effortlessly, with enthusiasm and anticipation.

Soon we disappeared into the clouds, into a special secret place, an open area that was warmly lit. The space expanded out among the clouds for as far as I could see. Gold tones were apparent, but the soft lighting seemed to be whatever color it needed to be for the children. Quiet harp music played in the distance. Just entering the space brought a surge of warmth to my heart that overtook my body. As we entered, the children all seemed to know what was in store for them. Each went to an angelic person who lifted the child onto his or her lap. The children were rocked, sung to, and allowed to bask in the warmth of love that permeated the entire space. There was the fragrance of flowers throughout and warmth that seemed to expand from the glow within each person. The warmth washed over the children, bathing their hearts and souls.

I was rocking a small girl. I felt extreme love pouring from my heart and settling into hers while we rocked. My arms embraced her, allowing her head to lie softly against me. Her body relaxed as she gave herself over in complete trust. I recalled how rocking my own children would often bring out a desire to rock them forever, never let them go. This was how I felt at this moment, rocking this little girl.

My eye caught sight of another child being rocked. I had to look again because the child I was seeing was me. I was about seven years old, wearing the same outfit I had worn the day I rocked myself in my miniature chair and wanted my mom to hold me and comfort me. And now I was being comforted. The angelic person holding me looked very much like my mother. As I rocked the little girl who was in my lap, I allowed my heart to emit a deep love for her. And as I was rocked, I allowed my heart to receive the deep love coming from the being who held me.

The light that had been soft when we entered the room grew as our hearts opened to give more and more love. Each of us allowed the glow to seep into our cells, our bodies, and our minds. The radiance of each child grew and merged with all of the others. Soon we were lost in light that made it appear that we were all one person, one being. And we were, because we could feel each other's pain and we could feel each other's joy as if it were our own pain and our own joy.

As dawn began to peek through the clouds, all the children gathered and we began our journey home. Before leaving, I was handed a blank scroll by the Star Angel. The children were guided back down the golden path to their beds, where they awoke to the start of a new day. I would later learn from the Medicine Woman that on this scroll I was to write healing words: a song, a book to help the children.

As I woke to the cold rain on my tarp, I realized that I was still radiating with the loving glow. I became aware, once again, of my cold body.

The song came to me again, prodding me to release the words, the tune, and the message to the world. In the cold of my sleeping bag, as I continued to shiver, I sang. It was a song from my heart, a song from above, a song for me, a song for the children.

> Hold the children close to you.
> Wrap your arms around them.
> Rock and sing and hold them close.
> Hold them in your arms.
>
> Lay their heads upon your breast.
> Let their hearts beat one with you.
> Hold them tightly in your arms
> Until they can remember.
>
> Teach the children they are loved.
> Teach the children there is hope.
> Teach the children they can trust.
> Teach the children how to feel.
>
> Peace, you children, you are loved.
> Peace, you children, you are loved.
> Peace, you children, you are loved,
> Unconditionally.

Peace, my child, I love you so.
Peace, my child, I love you so.
Peace, my child, I love you so,
Unconditionally.

As I sang, I allowed my body to sink into the bosom of Mother Earth and envisioned Father Sky reaching down to pick me up and look into my eyes, holding me tightly. I could feel the embrace of nature all around; the trees, the wind, and the earth were touching me, body and soul. And I recalled the same sense of love in experiencing my vision of rocking the children and being rocked myself.

Yes, my body was cold. Physically, I felt miserable. But my heart, my soul, and my spirit all felt extreme warmth and love that could comfort my cold body. And I knew that the vision was important because each of us could heal our wounds. Each of us could reach inside and learn to give ourselves what we needed to be whole and complete.

My soul trembled. I wondered, what was this deep need, this deep longing to be held, to be nurtured, to be loved? I sighed as I realized that this ever-embracing love was the ultimate gift from nature. The song continued to spring from my soul.

Peace my child, I love you so.
Peace my child, I love you so.
Peace my child, I love you so
Unconditionally.

I am Mother Earth beneath.
Hear my heart beat one with you.
Let me hold and rock you now.

Finding the Peace

Let me cuddle close to you.
Let me wrap you tightly
In this blanket, warmly.
Lay your head upon my breast
As my arms caress you.
Let me hold you, rock and sing,
As I 1 love you so.

Peace, my child, I love you so.
Peace, my child, I love you so.
Peace, my child, I love you so,
Unconditionally.

I am Father Sky above.
See my arms stretched way beyond.
Let me reach down, pick you up,
Bring you close as my arms close.
Let me wrap you tightly
In this blanket, warmly.
Lay your head upon my breast.
Hear my heart beat one with you.
Let me hold and rock you now.
Let me sing and cuddle close.

Peace, our child, we love you so.
Peace, our child, we love you so.
Peace, our child, we love you so,
Unconditionally.

Tell the children of the world,
Tell the little ones,

Tell them they are loved so much,
Tell them there is hope.

Teach the children of the world,
Teach the little ones,
Teach them they are loved so much,
Teach them there is hope.

Hold the children close to you.
Wrap your arms around them.
Rock and sing and hold them close.
Hold them in your arms.

Lay their heads upon your breast.
Let their hearts beat one with you.
Hold them tightly in your arms
Until they can remember.

Teach the children they are loved.
Teach the children there is hope.
Teach the children they can trust.
Teach the children how to feel.

Peace, you children, you are loved.
Peace, you children, you are loved.
Peace, you children, you are loved,
Unconditionally.

Peace, my child, I love you so.
Peace, my child, I love you so.
Peace, my child, I love you so,
Unconditionally.

It was done. I lay quietly. My mind was empty.

After a time, when it felt like more than two rainy days had passed, the Medicine Woman finally called to me. I rustled myself from beneath the tarp and looked to see if I were dreaming once again. But it was truly time: the Medicine Woman had come to take me off the hill. I eased out of my sleeping bag, waiting for circulation to return so I could stand. I allowed the Medicine Woman to embrace me as my body melted into hers. I was crying, but this time for joy.

The Medicine Woman moved quickly as she put most of my things into the center of the tarp, then wrapped them up into a bundle that would be retrieved later. My pipe and altar relics were to go with me now. Although I moved slowly, I felt whole. With the Medicine Woman supporting me, we walked carefully down the hill through the trees.

I was guided into the sweat lodge where I took a seat next to the Medicine Woman. She called for rocks to warm me, and the sweat lodge soon began to fill with heat. One of the supporters passed in dry clothes through the doorway. I shed my cold, wet clothes, peeling them away from my skin as I slipped into the warmth awaiting me. The dry clothing clung to me and seemed to embrace me.

As I cradled a cup of hot tea in my palms, my fingers began to tingle. I sipped it while the Medicine Woman handed me the meal that would break my three-day fast: honey, yogurt, and brown rice. The first bites entered my body with a magnified sensual awareness. A comforting warmth enveloped my body, now from both inside and outside. I felt loved.

Sitting cross-legged next to the Medicine Woman on the dry ground, I looked down. I didn't want to talk. I didn't want to interact. I felt somewhat intruded upon. I didn't know if I was ready to come back into the world.

I slept soundly that night in the shelter of my tent, opening the top flaps so I could look up and see the stars. Night came and went without incident, and I awoke early to the morning dew on my sleeping bag. The birds were singing their morning greetings.

I lay there remembering the day before: the day in the rain, the completion of the song, the depths of my feelings, my despair. As I thought about the song, I decided I had to go back to my spot, my vision quest place, to be there with my song one last time. The song's words were clear in my head but the tune didn't roll off my tongue. Although the thought of losing the song panicked me a bit, I also realized that my concern was symbolic of my whole life. I had always struggled to trust myself, my own knowing, my ability to carry the tune.

I rose, threw on some clothes, and silently left the campsite. I didn't want to meet anyone, didn't want to talk. My sanctuary seemed a lot closer today, and I arrived within minutes. I welcomed the quiet that allowed me to hear more clearly, allowed me to shut out the rest of the world, allowed me to hear myself.

The sun was radiant, with a beauty that often follows after rain has finished its work of washing and nourishing nature. I felt its warmth, its joy, its freshness, and my heart swelled. There was a knowing here, and I needed to grasp it. The knowing was all about the song, about my beat, my tune.

Guided, I got up off the ground and raised my arms in gratitude. I felt the sun spread into my heart, and I began to dance. It didn't matter that I stumbled at first. I was alone, and I was working, working to hear the tune clearly and to dance the steps accordingly.

I lifted my feet and let them land where they would. They picked up speed. I twirled, letting myself hear the beat, the beat of the song, the beat of the words, the beat of the work, the beat of my soul. I felt as if I had been lifted out of a deep fog and suddenly my whole life made sense. Dancing to my own song seemed to be natural as long as I just let it happen without thinking about it. And as my fog continued to lift, my dance steps lightened even more.

It had been ten years since I began the process of listening to myself, of trying to live authentically. I had been practicing the steps for a long time. I recalled a time about six months after I was out of the hospital, how I had wanted to celebrate my new dance steps, the new me, my birthing, but no one seemed to be celebrating with me. No one was happy about my changing the dance steps to align with the new tune within me. That was fitting somehow, because I had to step into my own knowing, even though others were not approving or supporting me. This was something that was hard for me to do.

I had written a poem that expressed my surprise and sadness when the world was not celebrating my birthing.

> I'm here
> Where's the band?
> I don't hear the music
> Doesn't someone want to dance with me?
> Let's celebrate . . .
>
> There is no music
> There is no band

The dance is within
And I'll have to practice
The steps with me . . .

It's okay, world—
Join me when you can
In the meantime I'll practice my dance
And know the steps
That go with my tune within—
For truly,
I cannot share the music
Or dance
Until I can do my part
Of the dance steps to my very own tune!

How wonderful a gift to be blessed with the realization that my song, my work, my life were all in order. To realize that when I listened to my own tune, the steps were like a dance, light and easy. The sun shone down on me, warming me, lighting my soul.

I headed back toward the campsite. Somehow, coming down off the hill and out of my own little world felt like the low point of the vision quest. As I recalled my profound sadness on the hill—the moments when I had gone beyond the depths of my sobs and lay motionless, without energy or emotion, soaked and chilled—I realized it might have actually been the high point. I could understand that reliving the pain of my infancy allowed me to release it, and having gone through the release of my old pain was a gift. And for that I was grateful. There was a part of me thankful to have completed my journey in this vision quest; yet another part of me knew I had tasted something that couldn't be attained in my everyday life. It was the intimacy of going deep within myself—of journeying with the Great Spirit and the ancient ones, grandfathers, grandmothers—while seemingly alone. Never had I felt so full, so loved, so cared about while being physically by myself. I smiled. I never thought I could find that part of myself. And I knew that I really loved who I was.

Epilogue

Although I rarely took days off just to stay home, a quiet day seemed mandatory after the last few days on the hill, and I was grateful that I hadn't scheduled any appointments.

Jerry went to work; the kids went to school. I was able to be alone, which felt like a gentler way to transition back. I drank hot tea, journaled, reflected on the past few days, and tried to put the pieces of my life together. What had led me to this point?

Looking back, I felt awed by the presence of Spirit in my life. Once again, I realized there were no accidents in life. I had gone to school after I had been hospitalized, after I had begun my own dance to my own tune. My desire was to become a therapist, a person who could sit with others who were struggling, to guide them inward just as Mona had guided me. And I loved it, loved sitting with people as they worked to heal and become whole. I loved the unlimited potential that would open up for them.

At first, I had thought I might work only with women, but my focus had expanded when I started counseling children with attachment disorders. This hadn't been something I set out to do; nor was it something I wanted to do. But life had brought it to me, had made it happen.

I recalled the first child with whom I worked years ago, right after I graduated. Sara had been living with her biological mother, who neglected her. Eventually she was placed in foster care.

Sara was so wounded. She helped me understand the rage and hurt in children who are not cared for the way they need to be during their early years; many have a very difficult time ever trusting anyone. I knew children needed to be held, rocked, and nurtured. I worked to help these damaged children accept this warmth in their lives, unfold, and allow it when it seemed to come too late.

I thought of my own journey, my pain, my depression, my sense of hopelessness; how I had finally been able to make changes that worked for me, that allowed me to dance to my own inner tune; and how without the depression, I might never even have heard my own tune.

During the vision quest, there had been times when my sobs, my cries, were for the children with unmet needs, the human condition, the children I worked with, the children like Sara. From those times came the verse about the children of the world. This verse had been about my work: of helping parents to hold and rock their children; of helping the children to feel safe and to learn they could sometimes trust the world; and of the joy of watching a child become soft and whole again.

Sometimes it was a good day in therapy, but sometimes it was not. Then I would just give the parents the support and encouragement they needed to continue to do what they needed to do for the sake of their child, for one more day. Maybe the family had merely made it through another week of raising the child. I had to focus on the small victories at times.

My song validated my inner guidance. It validated the work I tried not to do, yet always came back to when there was a child who needed healing. There was a message in the song for me to pay attention: my path was my destiny.

My journey seemed a bit haphazard. But was it really? I grew up in a family that was emotionally distant although I was well cared for physically. I was a sad child, depressed throughout my life, although I didn't even know it. I wanted connection with my family.

I had to chuckle a bit at the obvious within myself. I believed fully that there are no accidents in life. That the experiences, people, and the lessons all come because, on a soul level, our souls call to them for us to grow and become more whole. No wonder I took great pleasure in setting that up for parents to do with their children. No wonder I felt such a pull, so much passion to help these children be connected to someone.

I loved doing therapy with others for lots of reasons. The connecting that happens in the therapeutic relationship when people become very real with themselves always feels reverent. Through that process, the deep relationship that is developed enables a client to heal and change. I loved that work. I loved the honor of walking the Red Road with a client.

But the work with children who allowed no one into their hearts, that was different because it focused on helping children be real and open to their parents or caregivers or whoever was their support. The relationship didn't happen between the children and me; instead I, as the therapist, facilitated the joining of the children to their support.

I was drawn to do this work, but I struggled with it. There was great satisfaction, but it was also really hard and sad. The children didn't want to do the work; they were difficult. The parents were usually exhausted and ready to give up. I often watched a child unravel everyone in the family to the point that the family was falling apart. Much as I tried not to be working in this area, I always found myself in the midst of it. And then there was the song that came to me about the children. It seemed to be my calling.

The vision quest had been the validation of my life's journey. Once again I gave thanks to the heavens, to the Great Spirit, and to the grandfathers and grandmothers, and I hoped that I could own my calling even when it felt overwhelming and when I found doubt in myself. I gave thanks to my parents who did the best they knew how, and I gave thanks to my children that they would know that I did the best I knew how, and I gave thanks to Spirit that all was in perfect order. I breathed and allowed breath to encompass me.

———m———

Back at work, I walked out into the waiting room to greet my first client. We went into my office, and as the client got comfortable, I shut the door. With that click of the door came the awareness of something mystical. We were entering the beginning of the hour of potentiality, not knowing what lay ahead but always knowing it was important.

Acknowledgments

I acknowledge my parents, who are the perfect parents for what my soul called in for my life. Because of you, I am who I am today. Thank you for being there for me as we grew together and as we continue to make our relationship a priority filled with love.

To my brother, Pat, who spent countless hours processing my inner thoughts and book ideas, and reading the different versions of this book. I am grateful for your unending support, your understanding of who I am, and your consistent encouragement to go for the gold. Your friendship means more than I can put into words. And to Lisa, my sister-in-law, who quietly supports my closeness with Pat and has become a sister to me. Thank you for reading the manuscripts, giving me feedback, and mostly for believing in me.

To my supporters, Seanne, Vicki, Loyie, and Jamie, thank you for showing me the reflection of full acceptance of myself. It was through your embracement that I became more solid in who I am.

To my therapist, Mona Schroeder, thank you for putting your arms around me and holding me. Your touch gave me the priceless gift of learning how to connect with myself.

To my dear friend Deb England, who journeyed with me to the fruition of this book. Thank you for enduring the hours of reading my manuscripts and your gentle ways in giving me feedback and teaching me about writing.

I am very grateful to my friend Bob, who has encouraged me each step of the way in manifesting a completed manuscript. And to my mentor, Larry Shapiro, who made this final process seem so simple and just encouraged me to get on with it. Your motto of "just do it" really changed my perspective of publishing a book. And to my editor, Karen Schader. Karen, your professionalism, your skill, your ability to edit to my style of writing was impeccable. You got me over the finish line.

To my children, Jeremy, Jessica, and Jacquelyn: You have been my greatest teachers. It is my love for you that has given me countless opportunities to change and become a better person. May your journey to the depths of your soul be rewarding and encourage you to continue to be all you are—as the essence of each of you is enough.

And finally, to my husband, Jerry: I thank you for your unwavering faith in my ability to write this book and for your total acceptance when I spent weekends upon weekends just writing. Your consistent behind-the-scenes support spoke loudly of your love and commitment to me these past thirty-five years.